The Little Dog
That Could

FILIPPO VOLTAGGIO

Cover Photo: Ciccina
Courtesy of Laura De León

Author Photo by Peter Jandula-Hudson

Cover and Book Design by Marnie Tenden

ISBN: 0692568212
ISBN-13: 9780692568217   LIFE CHANGES Publishing

DISCLAIMER

This book retells an experience as lived and interpreted by the author. Many of the practices related within, when understood and applied, could assist people in creating extraordinary lives for themselves and others.

While written for informational and even transformational purposes, the healing practices realized in this story are not intended to be a substitute for professional medical advice, diagnosis, or treatment. Experiences and results in this true story are not typical.

For people and pets with medical and/or psychological conditions, it is advisable to seek out appropriate advice from qualified professionals.

DEDICATION

This book is dedicated to my nieces and nephews, Antonino, Fiorella, Lilianna, Gabriella, Marco, Chiara for helping remind me of the magic I had long forgotten since becoming an "adult."

CONTENTS

INTRODUCTION

I have often heard said by people, phrases like, "the answers are right in front of you." In the Taoist tradition it is said that "the teacher appears when the student is ready." Recently I heard, "the way we do anything is the way we do everything." Oh, and then there's this one, "The answers are all in the 'NOW!'" I could go on and on. For some reason, I kept running across these phrases and accumulating them in my memory banks and they had become stuck in my head.

Ever since I was a child, I was always naturally inquisitive and would ask a lot of questions of my family and friends. At times I would be met with these phrases as answers. For a time, I wasn't sure what was bothering me more, the fact that I didn't have the direct answers to my questions or that I didn't understand what meaningful friends, authors and teachers where trying to say to me by way of these phrases as answers.

What did all this mean? What does all this mean? As if the questions I was asking weren't puzzling enough, the riddles I got as answers I felt were sending me on a mental treasure hunt. "The answers are right in front of you?" Where? In front, where? "The teacher appears when the student is ready." "I'm ready! Teach me!" I would sometimes say to people who said that to me.

When I was a child I had a "toy" called a Chinese Torture. It was a tube made of straw. I would put my forefingers in the tube's openings, one on each side. The straw was entwined in such a way, that once the fingers were in, I couldn't get them out. The harder I tried to get my fingers out, the harder the tube wrapped itself around my fingers, which made it impossible to get my fingers out.

The more agitated I got about not being able to get my fingers out, the more the tube pinched my fingers and clung to them. Ironically, in the midst of the confusion and frustration that this, seemingly harmless tube brought on, the answer was to "relax." As I later learned, if I relaxed, the tube would easily slip off my fingers.

Many years later, as an adult I reflected upon that exercise and discovered what a brilliant analogy it was for life. Sometimes, in our most agitated state, we can't get out of a mess into which we have gotten ourselves. And the more we get frustrated, angry, or pull or push harder or stronger, the more the very situation we are trying to get ourselves out of, wraps itself around us and hurts us and angers us and confuses us all the more.

As much as I still fight it, I have learned that the answer to many situations is to "relax," let go. As with the "Chinese Torture," wherein I needed to relax my muscles, so too, in life, when we relax our mind, our position on a certain situation, or expectation, or if we let go of our fear or anger around a particular experience... the answer often comes. The problem might, "slip off our fingers," like the Chinese Torture, and out of our lives forever.

Interestingly, the Chinese Torture wasn't something I put down, once I figured it out. It provided much fun, not only sharing it with other children and adults, but for myself as well. I would wrap it around my forefingers and purposefully make it grip me as I pulled hard, just to get the sensation. Then eventually, I would relax and it would loosen. I would then do it again, and again. Extrapolating into "real" life, sometimes when we have finally "figured it out," we put ourselves in a similar situation to be gripped and tightened maybe to prove to ourselves that we could slip out of it just as easily the next time, or maybe this is part of the experience of life as we know it.

I'm sorry to say that it took several tries to be able to slip in and out of the tube with ease, because the second or third time, I still wanted to revert back to my old ways of doing and force my way out of the situation. Hmm, what an analogy for life, right? So just because you finally "get it," doesn't mean that we won't put ourselves into the exact or very similar situation again, or we won't bring whatever it was on again. In this way, we are either testing ourselves, making sure that we have learned something, or sometimes, it could be a habit or pattern we have gotten into that we haven't yet broken.

To carry on the analogy of the "Chinese Torture," toy, when a bunch of us children would be watching others struggling about with the tube attached to their fingers and not being able to get out of it, some children had to try it too, because they thought they knew better. Of course, the first time any of us tried it, we made all the same mistakes that the person before us made, even when they finally had figured it out, we still had to try it, "our way," or the way that came "natural" to us. And what was "our way?" What was "natural?" More often than not, it was the same old way we had been doing things in the past, or had seen our parents do, or other children or adults around us do, even though we had just seen it not work with our own eyes.

Sound familiar? Does this sound like anyone you know? Does this sound like anything you have done? This was me. I'd like to think this is no longer the way I operate in the world, but this too is a process. Welcome to my world.

The answers started coming in various forms, in teachers I never would have considered teachers, experiences I never imagined I would have had, and in ways that, to say the least, were in no way expected.

One such teacher came in a small package and it is to this teacher that I owe much gratitude. Like her, this book is little, but like her, this book packs a wallop of life lessons and insights that if you are ready, like I finally truly was, could change your life for the better.

Enjoy the journey ahead and look for the answers to the questions in your own life, because they might just be right in front of you. And the teacher you've wanted might finally appear, it might even be Ciccina by way of this book!

1 MY LIFE WAS NEAT

I wouldn't describe myself as a clean freak, although some people might. But I do have some of the traits that a person described as such would have. I remember getting into arguments with a friend because she wanted to place a pillow from the couch onto the floor of my clean living room carpet so she could sit on it. A no, no, to be sure in my house, even though, in her opinion, the floor was clean enough. Worse, one evening, a friend went and got a pillow from my bed to try and do the same thing. That was not a fun evening to say the least. She just couldn't understand, and I just couldn't understand how she just couldn't understand.

When I lived in a smaller place, at parties at my house, I would find friends lying, talking on my bed. First of all, I didn't want anyone in my bedroom, much less on my bed, period. Secondly, my comforter was all white and so that did not go over well with me. But thirdly, the comforter was a down comforter, and when people lie on down, it crushes the feathers. I couldn't understand why people didn't know this and furthermore, when I informed them, of this, why they didn't respect it.

Then there were the friends that would bring their pets over to my house without asking permission. What? I think some of them didn't ask because they knew what the answer would be. Imagine my surprise when I would find a cat sitting on my comforter or better yet, buried in my pillows on my bed. Imagine my angst

1

when friends would beckon their dogs to jump up onto my new beige fabric couch to sit with them. Then there are the friends that would bring their dogs' toys with them and allow their dogs to plop their slobbered on toys on my couch.

One thing that really got me was when they would reach into my cupboard and just grab one of my plates or bowls, especially when they would be part of a set that I would use for special occasions, and fill them up with water or food and place them on the floor for their pet. Okay, let's face it; it bothered me, no matter what plate they used, these were people plates and did not belong on the floor. I ate out of them I didn't want dogs or cats eating out of them. Didn't anybody agree with me on this?

I can't say that I enjoyed any of these experiences or for that matter the arguments that came afterwards with friends and family who just didn't understand my point of view on this subject matter.

Oh, and then there were the friends who wanted to use things in the house that in my opinion were just for decoration. I actually had a friend bring over flowers once and try and use an expensive crystal vase that was, in my opinion, only supposed to be decorative, as a vase for her flowers. That did not go over well for either one of us.

It wasn't like people had to take their shoes off before they walked in the house, not that I think there is anything wrong with that, I kind of still think that is a good idea. And I really didn't have many rules. But there were some traits that I possessed that I began to see would drive some people crazy. In my view of my life, they were well justified and the way I thought about things was the way I wanted to think about them, or so I thought.

For example, since I am on a roll, if friends came over and tried to cook in my kitchen I would clean up after them while they were cooking. Or if I had a guest or guests, and they were the only ones using the guest bathroom, I would clean the guests' bathroom often during their stay. Okay, I have to admit, that's a little crazy, now that I think about it.

I remember a friend trying to use an ice bucket and filled it with water to do something or other, I don't know what, but it was the decorative ice bucket, not the one that was supposed to be used as an ice bucket. This particular ice bucket was made of crystal. I had another ice bucket that was made of plastic. I still think that common sense says the crystal ice bucket could break under the weight of the water, or being carted around by its decorative handles. But in any case, my way of thinking wasn't open to negotiations, at the time, and I came to learn it often didn't serve me or others.

As my friends and family members started to have children, you could imagine their angst when they were coming over to my place for a visit. It got to the point where one of the parents would hold the child or children outside, while the other parent would walk in my place and child proof the whole place, not necessarily just to protect their kids, but also to keep peace in the family/friendship.

Though I am not exaggerating any of this, the litany of these incidents is disproportionate because this wasn't something that occurred every day, or every moment of the day. For the most part, my friends and I had reached a comfortable way of being together when it came to being in my house. Although, for the most part, we spent more "being" time at their houses and that made it more comfortable for everyone.

Finally, let's talk about my car. Why, because the car is relevant. In fact, this is all relevant. Honestly, I didn't set out to write a "tell all" book about myself. For that matter, I didn't set out to write a book at all, until the following story "happened" to me. In order for some of my "lessons," or "answers," to make sense to those who don't know me, or who didn't know me then, some things need to be put into perspective.

Thus my car is relevant because my car was as clean as my house. Nothing in my car was out of place and one thing I didn't dare do was to eat or drink in it. When I first started driving, I didn't have the guts or confidence to tell people that they couldn't smoke in my car, but I would smell it and hate it for months later and kick myself for not stopping them. The same thing would happen regarding friends and their pets. When I would go somewhere with friends who had pets, so help me if they didn't always want to bring them along. There were times that no matter what excuse I came up with, I would "lose," and I would end up with animal hair everywhere, dirt on my seats and slobbered windows. Yup, that's how I saw it.

Oh, I almost forgot, one more thing, clothes. I used to care about clothes, in the sense that I liked clothes. I still like clothes, but I liked them most especially when they were clean and new and liked to keep them that way. On rare occasions, friends would ask if they could borrow a particular jacket or suit, like a tux, or something, and I would invariably say no. Just as invariably, they would argue and I would tell them that I didn't think they would keep the garment as clean as I would or treat it like I would and that was the reason I didn't want them to borrow it.

If it were a sports jacket, for example, would they fold it inside out when they took it off before placing it down so it wouldn't get dirty? Would they hang it up as soon as they were near a hanger to keep the jacket from wrinkling more than necessary? Would they be careful if they were eating to keep food, especially wine and oil away from my clothes?

Some of this my father taught me and I still agree with it to this day, but I guess, I had to learn to weigh it out with the quality of life and experiences and living, and all this was about to change, well, much of it. There's so much more I could share but this is enough to paint the necessary picture.

2 THE NIGHT I MET HER

It had been quite an eventful night already with my having gone to a gala and had been acknowledged by and had my picture taken with some of the "Who's Who" of Hollywood and politics. I was feeling pretty good about myself. I was driving home in my fairly new and very clean Mercedes Benz, dressed in my black silk pants and black silk pressed shirt, with very few wrinkles on it despite having been worn all evening, and my black suede jacket.

I had actually arrived home and had parked the car when the thought came over me that I needed/wanted to have some munchies before the night was over. Since it was late and I knew that I shouldn't be eating munchies, and of course, I was craving the kind that are the worst for my health and my waistline, I convinced myself that I could have munchies if I bought the kind that came from the health food store near my house.

That store closed at 10 PM and I noticed that it was 9:30 PM, so since the store was only five minutes away by car, I would make it just fine and I would be able to have my "healthy" munchies. I lived on a busy street that had four lanes, two in each direction. It was a very well traveled road, including city buses, at any time of the day or night. This particular night was no less busy than any other night. And as I was driving down the road on a mission to get my munchies from the health food store, dressed to the nines, I gasped at the sight of a little, little dog all by him or herself, trying

5

to cross this four lane street.

How I noticed her in the dark, a distance away on the sidewalk, I will never know. She was shorthaired, had no reflective collar, and was black, tan and grey in color. Spotting her was not easy. But as soon as I spotted her, my heart went to my throat as I noticed her looking across the road, just knowing what she was thinking. I might have even blurted out to myself in the car, "Please don't cross." Just as I was thinking that, she started making a zigzag attempt to cross the road.

I immediately put on my flashers as a way of alerting the other drivers that they should pay attention to something going on, in the road ahead. While I held my breath and slowed my car down, this little, little dog dodged cars that were unfortunately oblivious to him or her and landed itself miraculously unscathed on the sidewalk on the other side of the street. I was happy that the dog had made it but was concerned that A) the dog was undoubtedly lost, afraid and alone; and B) that the dog might try and cross the road again. I pulled over to the side of the road and for a moment, watched the dog from across the street.

Surprisingly, the dog looked right back, in fact, directly at me. As I write this, it surprises me all over again, because at that point, I was on the other side of this four lane street from the dog, and I felt like the dog was looking right at me, and not even for a second diverting its gaze. I thought to myself, that if I can get my car across the road and into the nearest driveway without killing myself, I could rescue the poor little thing. I even heard myself say, in my head, as I was looking at the beaming eyes of the dog, before attempting to cross the street, if I come over there, please, "come to me," let me help you.

"Come to me?" What was I going to do with a dog? It was as if I was having a conversation in my head with the dog and with myself. As if someone was giving me the answers in my head, I thought I heard "Take her to Laura." Laura was a dear friend of mine who was so wonderful with animals. For sixteen years or so, she had two dog companions, whom she had rescued, and whom had both passed away within the past six months, a few months of each other. This had happened so recently that I knew she wouldn't be ready for a dog and besides, I argued in my mind, this dog probably had a collar with the owner's name and number on it, and the owner would surely be happy to have him or her back.

These and many more thoughts ran across my mind, most of them telling me to just leave, because there was no way I could really help. Other thoughts included facts, like the health food store closed at 10 PM and because of this stop, I had less time to get my munchies and get home after a long, big day and evening. But a voice stronger than all the others won out and I maneuvered my car into the driveway of an apartment complex, across the street closest to the dog.

For some silly reason, I envisioned this "rescue" to be not only quick and easy, but like a scene from a fantasy film. I pictured the dog immediately running toward me, wagging its tail, its tongue hanging out, and barking in doggy talk, "My savior, my savior, you have come." So because of this "vision," I just parked my car with the back of my car still partially in the middle of the street and the front of it completely blocking the driveway and potentially anyone who would want to enter or exit this apartment complex's parking structure.

I even left the car running, put the car in park and opened the car door and started saying, "Come." The dog just looked at me. "Come." And still the dog just looked at me. I got out of the car and stood by the car and this time tried another approach. I asserted myself and commanded, "COME!" Still the dog did not come. I wondered, did this dog not know how hard this was for me and how I clearly did not know what I was doing but I was doing it all for him or her?

About this time I noticed that another car had stopped too and a young male and female couple ran out of the car to rescue the dog as well. "Wait a minute," I thought to myself, "I am the dog's rescuer, I have this situation under control. You can go home now." But I didn't say that out loud. Out loud I said, "Hi, is this your dog?" "No, we just saw it while it was crossing the street. We have to get it to safety. We can't just leave it on the street like this." the young lady said.

Just as the young lady was finished speaking, in the blink of an eye, the dog started running toward me really quickly. I moved aside in case it was used to jumping in cars, clearly not thinking like my "usual" self at that moment, and made way for the dog to jump to safety. But instead of jumping into my car, this little dog ran right under my car. When I crouched down to look at the dog, (careful not to rest my knees on the cement sidewalk and chance putting a hole in my silk pants), the dog had parked itself right in the middle of the car, and was trembling.

"Great!" I thought to myself. "Now how are we going to get it out?" Concerned for the dog, I immediately turned off the car, that was still half-way in the street and blocking a driveway, and put on the emergency break so the car wouldn't move while the dog was under it. The dog was right in the middle of the car, too far to reach from either side. We all tried. I tried grabbing the dog from one end and the couple tried grabbing the dog from the other at the same time, to no avail. Of course, I could have tried getting down on the sidewalk and squeezing myself under my car, but I didn't think so, I was wearing silk and suede after all. Did I mention the shoes? Never mind.

As we stood around trying to think of what to do, the young lady had an idea. She told her boyfriend to get a steak bone from their car in case they could lure the dog out with the smell. As her boyfriend went to get the steak bone, I had to ask, what they were doing driving around with a steak bone in their car? The young lady explained that it was her Birthday and they were driving home from eating out and they had saved the bones from their steak dinners for their two dogs.

The boyfriend returned with steak bones and while he waved one of them under the car, both the girlfriend and I waited for the result of this potentially brilliant idea. When I crouched down to see what was happening, I didn't think the dog even tried to sniff the bone or the air to get a whiff of the bone. It just sat there looking one way, then the other, and God only knows what was going through its undoubtedly frightened little head. With the failing of the bone trick, the three of us stood and contemplated what would be our next strategy.

Every once in awhile I would glance at my watch and think, "Okay, I still have a few minutes to get to the health food store to get my munchies before they close." "Okay, I still have a couple minutes to get to the health food store before they close, and once I'm in, they'll let me shop even if they're closed." "Okay DOG! You are really trying me now. I better not miss getting my munchies at the health food store because of you!"

As I stood there talking to the couple, at one point the young lady got down on her knees and tried her hand at getting the dog, by herself. The young man and I started making idle chatter since I, at least, had nowhere I could go with a dog under my car. He started telling me about their dinner and where they lived and...

All of a sudden we heard the young lady call out, "It's a GIRL!" as if the belly of my car had given birth to a puppy or something. Both the boyfriend and I crouched down on our side of the car looked down and across. To our amazement, the girlfriend was sitting on the sidewalk on the other side of the car, coddling the dog as if in fact she were a newborn and the dog was wagging her tail in excitement as if everything was finally all right.

"Honey, we gotta take her," said the young lady to her boyfriend. "I know, I was thinking the same thing," he responds. "Wait a minute, she's supposed to come with me," I hear inside my head. To which I start arguing with myself again, inside my own head. "And what exactly am I supposed to do with her?" "Let them take her? If they do, I can still make it to the store."

I listened to the two "would be" rescuers argue as to how they can make this happen. Of course, we all were thinking that we would find the rightful owner soon and it would only be a matter of days. But even for a matter of days, we each thought we should take her. This surprised me more than anything. Here was my chance to have done my good deed for the day, and go, since I had important things to do before 10 PM. I could leave them to figure it out. After all, the young lady was holding the dog. It was as good as done.

As I debated in my head, the thought that I needed to take the dog home with me was ever growing stronger. Still the couple debated. This couple already had two dogs, and it seemed perfect because they could take care of one more dog more easily than I could take care of one. They already had food, leashes, dog bowls, what was one more dog? They then told me that the "problem" was that they had a roommate who also had a big, big dog and that they literally were afraid it would eat the little dog for a snack.

We all crouched down to contemplate as we completely covered the little dog with our hands petting her and giving her love and attention, right there on the sidewalk. In an instant, the young lady stood up, breaking us out of our little moment. The boyfriend and I stood up as well and the next thing that happened, the girlfriend was handing me the dog. "What?" First of all, I am wearing a silk shirt with a black suede jacket. Can people not see? The dog could snag the shirt really easily, and it will shed all over my black suede jacket. Plus, the dog was probably dirty, not to mention it had been under my car, and could easily have oil on her... you can't clean suede that easily.

My mind was thinking one thing and I was watching myself do something else. I took the dog without objecting and immediately went and put her in my car. "Wait!" My thoughts continued. "Here is a dog, not even my dog, trampling on my new, clean leatherette seats. The dog probably got all greased and grimy under my car..." All the while I was carefully placing her in the car and closing the car door so she couldn't get out. "She might be a stray. For all I know she hadn't been bathed in weeks and probably has dirt, lice and fleas and who knows what else, and now they are all in my car!"

I went around the car to my newfound allies and tried to make a plan of action. The dog obviously did not have a tag identifying her current home; in fact, she didn't even have a collar. So, since they had dogs, and I never owned a pet except goldfish, as an adult, I asked them, how one went about finding the rightful owner and enlisted their help.

I explained to them that "we" needed to take care of this situation immediately because firstly, I lived in a complex that didn't allow pets, and I was doing this only because they couldn't take the dog home, so in essence, I was doing them a favor. So they had to help me, help them, help the dog, and besides, it would be fun, this would be our new friendship's "pet" project.

All the while the dog was looking at us perched up on my door armrest with her nose stuck to the window and her nose leaving a trail at every turn. I didn't know what to think and how to react. I reassured myself that it was only temporary and she wouldn't be in my car for very long, and I could take my car to the car wash first thing in the morning.

My new friends told me to check the lost dog section and also post to Craig's list, and that they would put up posters in the neighborhood, since they lived near where we found the dog. They went on to tell me to go to the local pet rescue and let them know I had the dog and to bring them a picture in case anyone called looking for their dog. With us doing all this, they were sure we would find the dog's owner within a week.

That seemed reasonable enough. "A week?" "Wait," I exclaimed in my head. I proceeded to tell them that we had to find the dog's owner sooner than a week. Besides living in a complex that did not allow animals, I had a busy life, I was hardly ever home, and I traveled extensively. Furthermore, I had not taken care of a pet nor did I have anything at home that would facilitate my taking care of a dog. Besides pet paraphernalia, I was also thinking I didn't have the mindset and skills to care for a dog. Not only that, to mention a beige coach, white comforter, very clean floors...

In my head, I was thinking of my schedule for the next day and the next couple of days and wondered how I would be able to add a dog and a dog's needs to my schedule. My "partners in rescue" assured me that they would be with me on this, jokingly implying "to help this bachelor with his newborn baby, as best they could." I believed them. We laughed, we exchanged numbers, we hugged and we parted ways.

I looked at my watch in anticipation of my previous "important" plans, and by the time this rescue was over, I had long missed my opportunity for munchies from the health food store by at least a half hour because of little Miss doggy. But ironically, munchies for me were the last thing on my mind at that point. I thought to myself, decidedly being a bit dramatic, "What if this poor little dog hadn't eaten in weeks?". In any case we had to remedy that right away.

3 OUR FIRST NIGHT

As I got in the car and sat down, the little sad doggy turned into happy doggy. She jumped in my lap and started licking my face. As you might imagine by now, I was not a big doggy kisses and doggy tongue in the face kind of guy. I gently picked her up off my silk pants and carefully pried her away from my silk shirt and black suede jacket, making sure her nails were not snagging any of my clothes, and placed her on my clean leatherette seats.

I then brushed my pants, shirt and jacket, just in case there was something left on them. While being fastidious, I was at the same time thinking that though I was stuck between a rock and a hard place, I was going to buck it up for the "good of the animal kingdom." After all, I was going to earn my "Good Deed Doer" badge that night even if it meant dirty clothes, dirty seats and a nose trailed passenger side car window.

Actually, what I did was place her on the floor of the car on the passenger side, but that only lasted a second and she was up on the passenger seat in no time. And by the time I had put the car in gear and was backing up into on-coming traffic, because of the way I had parked, she was on my lap again.

I resigned myself to the fact that I had no choice, and that the poor little thing had been through enough in one night. Letting her stay on my lap was not going to kill me and obviously meant so much to her. I figured I could visit the dry cleaner in the morning and that would be that.

But no, as if this dog had come to test my patience, she excitedly got up on her hind legs and perched herself on my door and started snail trailing my driver side window with her nose while she clawed at my silk pants with her untrimmed nails trying to maintain her balance and get the best outside view. This was not going to be a night I would soon forget. When safe to do so, I picked her up off my pants and placed her on the passenger seat again only to have her jump right back on my lap.

We did this over and over until I got tired of it. She had won and I let her have her way. By now I figured that she had probably already snagged my clothes and I would have to throw them away. I would have to have a full detail on my car, but that it would be a small price to pay for the joy this little dog seemed to be having, and admittedly was starting to give me.

At that point of resignation was when I decided to talk to the dog. Out of my mouth came all these nice things. I told her how precious she was and how I was going to take care of her until we found her owner, and things like that. I hadn't talked to a dog in awhile. But it wasn't like I was a stranger to it; it had just been a long time. Inside me there was a little smile that was wanting to happen and a voice that was saying, "Come on, admit it, this is kind of fun, isn't it?"

No time to admit having fun with this, I was on a more serious mission. I had arrived at the nearest mega grocery store that I knew would be open at that hour and had to find this little one some food. As if I knew she would understand me, I told her that I would be right back and that I was going to get her some good food. I cracked the window for her and started making my way toward the store.

When I got in the store, I had to find the aisle I normally would avoid, the one with pet food and supplies. When I found it, I was in for a surprise. Wow, what a selection of dog food. I wasn't sure how to pick. Since, when I buy food for myself, I avoid as many processed foods as possible, stay away from chemical additives and preservatives etc., I figured I would feed the dog similarly. I started to read all the labels as I do when I shop for myself.

What an arduous task this turned out to be, not only because there were so many to read, but also because the dog food had so many ingredients that I didn't want to feed her. It had become important to me all of a sudden to feed her the best food I could. On the one hand I thought to myself, had she not taken her sweet time figuring out that she was supposed to come with me, I would have made it to the health food store and we both would have had healthy treats tonight.

On the other hand, I was thinking, what if she is not used to eating like this? And why should I care, I would only have her for a short while anyway? What if I bought her the more expensive, healthier food and she didn't like it?

While all these thoughts were going through my head, a more urgent one came through. What if she is scared in the car all by herself, in the dark, and wondering what is happening? How would I explain to her, that it took so long because it was for her own good? And maybe leaving her alone after having just "rescued" her wasn't a good idea. What if she is scared and is chewing my seat?

And then came this idea. What if she pees and/or poops in my car, then what? That wouldn't be as easy to clean and then that would be a really fine mess I would have gotten myself into. Unnerved by these latter thoughts, I hurried myself along, quickly found the best food I felt I could get, paid for it, and rushed out to the car in hesitant anticipation of what I might find.

What I found was a little dog wagging its tail so happy to see me, it finally got a smile out of me, and to tell the truth I was happy to see her. I greeted her and then thoroughly checked the car to find that she had not peed, or pooped or chewed the seat; she had patiently waited to give me the love I deserved for being her "savior," taking her with me, and buying her food.

We drove home, her on my lap, as if we had done this for years. I live on that same busy street where only an hour and some minutes before, we had locked eyes for the first time. Being that I was so horrified to see her crossing it, I wasn't going to chance and trust that she would follow me up the stairs to the gate leading to my front door, especially since she had never been to my place before. So I carried her up to my gate and then my door, over the threshold into the place we would call our home for the next day or so until we found her owner.

The moment I put her down, she ran around the house excitedly checking out her new digs and then ran back as if to say, "This will do just fine." And off she went again only to come back and say, "I like it here." And off she went again. It was odd. It was as if I could read her mind. Either that, or I was just thinking this is what she was saying. Or, it was just obvious she was happy. In any case, she was happy with my place and her new temporary home.

I let her do her snooping around thing while I tended to taking care of her food needs. I went to the cupboard and got a little bowl, opened up a can of dog food, and put the food in the bowl. And then it hit me. This is the bowl out of which "I" eat. Well, there wasn't much I could do, the dog had to eat and I wasn't prepared with a designated dog bowl. I didn't keep much plastic in the house so I didn't really have anything else, and it was just for that night.

I took another bowl out of the cupboard and put some bottled water in it and placed it on the floor. "Bottled water for the dog?" I thought to myself. "Of course," I don't drink out of the faucet, I wouldn't let her drink out of the faucet. What was happening to me?

"Hey." I called for the dog but she didn't come. "It's dinner time" I called out, but she didn't come. "I got something good for you to eat. You are going to like it," I was saying as I walked around looking for her.

"NO!" I exclaimed. "NO! You can't sit there!" She was sitting all comfortable on my white down comforter right in the middle of my bed looking like the little princess she obviously fashioned herself to be. This would not work for me. I would not have it. This was trying me more than I was going to let her get away with.

Of course, at my exclamation, she jumped off the bed immediately, and I quickly had to make sure that all the dirt and hair was brushed off the comforter and the comforter fluffed back into shape before returning to tend to her. I closed the bedroom door and all the other doors so she would not get herself into anything else tonight. As I entered into the living room prepared to serve her Royal Highness her supper, I found her all snuggled up on my beige fabric couch with her nose snuggled up against my Chinese Silk embroidered pillows.

"NO!" I exclaimed once again, "No, you can't sit there." "Please don't make this hard on me," I begged. "Now, let's go eat." "Come on." I brushed the couch and fluffed the pillows while she watched, curiously, and then led her to her bowls on the floor in the dining room.

I waited and watched to make sure she ate and drank. For a moment I felt like my Italian Mother, making sure her child was eating. But no, she wasn't having it. She didn't eat anything at all. I then got a spoon, and yes it was the spoon I eat with from my flatware set, and I even tried to spoon feed her, to no avail.

Nothing I tried would get her to eat or drink. So, back to the kitchen I went to open up another kind of canned dog food to see if she would like that instead. But no, she wasn't having any.

When she had refused to eat the second can of food I had opened for her, I decided I shouldn't force her. I got to thinking that maybe she had an upset stomach from all the excitement of the night, or that she wasn't hungry because she was not used to eating late at night. There was always the possibility that she didn't like the food I had bought her, but I decided not to force it. I wouldn't want the food to disagree with her, and have her vomit in my place. So, I was done trying. At least, I thought I was done.

I decided that she wasn't the only one that had had a tumultuous night and that I needed some comfort food. So, my soul food of choice, being American of Italian Heritage, is pasta.

Growing up, my mother made pasta as the first course to precede the second course, usually meat or fish, everyday. My Mother made pasta so many different ways that if she wanted to, I bet she could make pasta everyday for a year and never repeat a recipe. That is, every day except Sundays, Sundays it was always pasta and red sauce. And sometimes on Fridays, pasta aglio e olio, that's garlic and oil (Extra Virgin Olive Oil from Italy). But I digress.

So here it was practically midnight and I was making myself some pasta. Honestly, I can't remember what kind or how I fixed it at this point, because, like my Mother, I too can make it, and do make it often, so many different ways. All I can say for sure is that it had garlic in it, and it was undoubtedly delicious.

I finally sat down at the table in front of my pasta, which at this point, I felt I had earned after all that I had done that night. But before I could eat, guess whom I thought of? I was contemplating how I was going to make a bed for her, where she would sleep, and how I would take her for a walk without a leash, in case she needed to do her business that night. I needed to take her out, because I wasn't sure if she was house trained and certainly didn't want her doing her business in my place.

As I was thinking, I interrupted my thoughts with a, "Why aren't I eating?" kind of question? As my fork hits the plate, who should come waddling up to me with her tail wagging and nose in the air and sniffing? Well it's none other than little Miss Comforter hugging, couch sitting, pillow nuzzling, finicky eating, doggy Princess herself.

She came up sniffing around the table and me as if she were interested in what I was eating. I couldn't imagine that this dog had been raised Italian like I had and wanted her pasta, at midnight, no less.

Looking at her sniffing the air and begging, my Italian heart and soul wanted to see her eat. I started to think that the smell of the food opened up her appetite, so I figured, when I was finished eating I would have her try the dry dog food, or the snacks I bought her.

But before I could put my first fork full of pasta in my mouth, I heard the sniffing again. As if I was reading her mind again, I was thinking she really wanted the pasta. So up into the cupboard I went again for yet another one of my bowls, and in it I put some of my pasta. I hadn't made all that much pasta, it being late and all, and not figuring I would be sharing it with anyone, much less the dog, but share I did. Now I started thinking, if she sniffs it and walks away, after getting her a bowl and giving her some of my pasta, I won't be happy.

She would not disappoint. Little Missy started eating the pasta as if she too had an Italian Mother and her Mamma used to make pasta for her too. If fact, she ate it so fast it seemed like she hadn't had it since she was a little girl. This I knew I was completely making up, but it was a funny narrative. I laughed and complimented her, just like my Mother would, when I would finish all my food. In fact, she not only ate everything in the bowl, she licked the bowl clean.

When we finished our plates of pasta, or anything, for that matter, my Mother would fill it up again until there was no more in the pot. Without thinking that I hadn't made much pasta for myself to begin with, I took another few forks full of the pasta from my bowl and put it into her bowl. Immediately, she went for it and I watched in disbelief as she ate it all again. Then she turned to look at me as if she wanted more.

Well, this was getting ridiculous. If I gave her any more, she would have eaten all the pasta I had prepared for myself. This after everything else she had put me through that evening already. What was I to do? The dog was obviously Italian, liked my cooking above all else, and was still hungry! I took a fork full of the pasta and ate it myself, so I could at least taste it, and then gave her the rest.

Wouldn't you know it, this time, she leaned down to the bowl, smelled it, must have decided she had had enough, and walked away. Great! Now MY pasta was in HER bowl, which used to be my bowl, and she was full and I was still hungry! What could I do, but laugh at the whole situation and go to bed hungry!

4 THE LITTLE ONE'S BEDTIME

I found some rope to make a makeshift leash so that I could take her out to do her business before we both got some long needed rest. I personally was hoping to get some work done before going to bed. I had forgotten all about work I needed to do until that moment. But the night was what it was, and I was trying to "be in the now" and "go with the flow." And if that meant I couldn't get my work done, maybe I wasn't supposed to do it that night. This was not my modus operandi, but I was willing to adopt it for a night.

In Italian, my parents used to tell me many sayings, one of which seemed appropriate at that moment. The saying is, "Ogni mali un veni pi nosciri." Actually, that's Sicilian, and it loosely translates into, "Not every bad thing comes to bother us." In other words, there is possibly something good in what otherwise looks to be bad.

So I was going with it. The dog and I walked around the block. When she had had enough, she led the way back home. She went up my stairs ahead of me, as if she knew exactly where she was going, waited for me to open the gate, and then tugged at me as she hurried right up to my door as if we had done this a thousand times before.

When we got inside and I started to take off her makeshift leash, I looked at her as if to say, "Who are you?" In fact, I might have even said it out loud, with an uncontrolled chuckle, come to think of it. I had this feeling like we knew each other, or already had a special bond, and that didn't seem possible since I definitely had never seen her before that night.

Whoever she was, she was sleeping with me tonight, and I had to find her a place to sleep. There was one thing I knew for sure, she wasn't sleeping with me, in other words, not in my bed. I decided I would put her in my office. I figured that there were fewer things in there that she could break or chew on. The office had a painted cement floor, so if she peed or pooped, it wouldn't seep into the hardwood like in the rest of the place. Furthermore, she would be the furthest from my room, which was the way I wanted it.

I gathered up some blankets and made her a little bed. I grabbed one of my stuffed animals and a worn shirt of mine, and laid them and her down on her new bed. Did it dawn on me that she was going to be sitting on "my" blankets and cuddling up to "my" stuffed animal and shirt? Whether it dawned on me or not, it didn't matter at that point? I turned into a caretaker and had a job to do. I felt a sense of responsibility to this little one and anything I could do to make her short stay with me comfortable, I would do. That is, I would do anything short of her getting into my room, which I knew would mean getting on my bed, and eventually, in her mind, getting in bed with me.

I stayed with her and pet her until she was comfortable and had quieted down. I then got up to leave, and make my way to the door. But she got up too. She was fine while I was sitting with her. But once I was up, she was up. This started a new game that I was determined to win. She'd get up; I'd put her down. She'd get up; I'd put her down.

Finally I just said, "Fine." I figured she could roam around the office if she didn't want to sleep, but I had work to do. Work that was looking more and more like it definitely wouldn't get done that night, but I still hadn't given up on it.

During the get up and put down game, I realized that I had to be faster if I wanted to get out the door without her being either in front of me, or at my heels. I finally made it to the door at one point and quickly closed the door behind me.

We all know what happened next. The saddest whimpering sounds I had ever heard came from the other side of the door. Those were the first noises, other than the sniffing I had heard come out of the little one and they were so sad. I couldn't take it. I had to open the door. As soon as I did, the noises stopped, but the game started all over again.

After some time, I decided I would just have to leave her to whimper. I figured I would try to work with an ear to her whimpering in the background and monitor her for a period of time. I earnestly sat down in the living room to work, but between her whimpering and the many thoughts that went through my head, it was impossible for me to work at that moment. Not to mention, at that point it was late, and it had been a long day, and night, and I was still hungry, and tired.

One of the thoughts that went through my head was that she probably should have water in the room. This of course meant that I had to go back in the office. I went to get her water bowl and brought it in to her room, (my former office, where I would have been working, or would have been done working by now). Again I was greeted with a very excited doggy, happy to see me, as she was each time when reunited after we had been momentarily parted.

I was determined that no matter how many tail wags, or how deep her puppy dog eyes looked into my eyes, or how much she whimpered, I was putting my foot down. After all, I was still the master of this house.

I closed the door and let her whine until she tired herself out. Feeling she had fallen asleep, I stopped fooling myself that I was working, put my work away, and finally went to bed. "Goodnight doggy!" I said to myself, "I'm happy you're here."

5 MORNING HAS BROKEN

Morning came early despite the fact that I had gone to bed late. There was something different about that morning that didn't want me to sleep any longer but to wake and to awaken to a brand new day. I jumped out of bed remembering that I was not alone. I had a guest in my home and in my life. I couldn't wait to greet this happy morning, and greet my guest, to whose needs I wanted to attend to before she attended to them in my office.

I opened the door to find her head up, eyes wide open and tail in gear as if to say, "What took you so long, you sleepy head?" I walked to her greeting her with every morning pleasantry I could think of and more than I had offered to anyone in a long time. I started to pet her and she started to lick. I was not ready for that this morning, and I pulled her away saying, "Let's not get too excited." I reminded myself that this was only temporary, both the good and the responsibility, but for the time being, we were going to make the best of it and live it out for all it was worth.

I remembered that she probably needed to relieve herself, and immediately the cynical thought occurred to me that she probably had left surprises in the office. But after looking around, I found that there were no such surprises of any kind. What a great dog she was, I thought, no surprises of the nasty kind, but many of the good ones. I was beginning to think this was not going to be such a bad experience after all.

The little one, my makeshift leash, and I, shuffled off outside to take care of business. She was busily and excitedly exploring her temporary "vacation home's" surroundings and I was busy trying to figure out what I was going to do on that day with her and the work I had originally planned to do. In my mind I had made my decision that one way or another I was not going to look at these circumstances as a problem, but rather as the right thing happening in my life for a good reason, whether I knew what the reason was or not.

Though I couldn't think of any particular good reason, I was intent on thinking that way and enjoying the moment to the best of my abilities. I had finally come to the conclusion, good or bad, happy or sad, everything in life is temporary. If I didn't like something, I should try and see the good in it, because at some point it would change so why only focus on the bad in the meantime? Similarly, if I liked something, I tried to enjoy it as much as possible because it was going to change anyway, whether I wanted it to or not.

I could only hope that in either case the change would be for the better, especially if I had anything to do with it. That was not how all things always ended up, but then again, I hadn't gotten the concept down completely, so how would I know if they had or hadn't? Maybe it was just the way I was looking at it all?

Like in this case. I had a moment of thinking, "I can't let this dog and her happenstance in my life slow me down, I've got so much to do today." Though that thought was there, I also was doing my best to stay in the moment, the moment being exactly what it was.

Eventually we made our way back into the house and that time, I grabbed another bowl out of my cupboard and tried serving her dry dog food for breakfast since the other two cans of dog food obviously were a no go. I also made a mental note that I had better run the dishwasher; otherwise I wouldn't have any more bowls with which to feed the dog. Technically, I could tap into my finer china, and use the bowls from that set, but that wasn't going to happen.

I left the doggy to her own devices after putting her bowl down and without having breakfast myself. I went to my office and started to check Craigslist and the address of the nearest animal shelter and a few other sites I thought would help me find her owner. No sooner had I sat down to start my research that I find the doggy looking up at me at my feet. I turned my chair around to give her attention and laughingly said "What?" out loud. Before I could get the whole word out, she jumped up to my face and landed on my lap, as if that was where she belonged. It was as if we had done this thousands of times. It felt as if we had known each other for much more than just a few hours, most of which were spent sleeping in different rooms.

She was licking her chops as if maybe she had had a bite to eat, at least so I hoped. After petting her a bit, I placed her back down on the floor. As I returned my attention back to my computer I was startled by a bark. It was usually very quiet around my place and to have such a loud unexpected, sound right next to me really startled me. It was her, she was barking at me. This was the first time I had heard her bark. Up until that moment, I hadn't heard anything come out of her except the whimpering, but that day I got a bark. It was actually the cutest bark, as if to say, "Hey look at me," kind of bark. I just had to laugh.

As I turned my chair to look at her and talk to her again, up she went on my lap again, like nobody's business. Only this time, she burrowed herself under my arm as if to say, "I'm staying so don't even try it." I did try it. "Why does she have to win all the time?" I thought to myself. "And how am I supposed to get any work done?" So, try as I may, she made herself into dead weight, and how a little body could weigh so much, all of a sudden, was beyond me.

"Okay, maybe if I leave my chair a little further from the desk than usual, we can both fit comfortably and she can stay where she is and I can still work," I thought. After all, I was working for her, trying to find her rightful owner and home, and how appropriate was it that she stayed right by me as we searched together.

Hours went by and I had had little luck on the computer in getting much more information. I called up my new friends and comrades I had met the night before. I left them a message. Later they called me back and told me they had placed "Dog Found" posters everywhere where they would be seen and assured me they were doing their part of the deal. I told them that I was on my way to the shelter and was going to take the dog with me instead of bringing them a picture.

Hours later the dog was still on my lap and when it was time to get up, the dog just didn't want to move. But it was time to get up and go do something. I had also pretty much E-mailed everyone on my To Do list and let them know that I would get to our appointments and deadlines, but that it might be later in the day. I let them know a little about what was going on, and told them that I had decided to take the morning and part of the afternoon, if necessary, to help my new little friend. Not only did I feel a sense of responsibility, but she was such a good dog, I felt for her, her owner who I assumed was missing her, and felt this really deserved my attention.

I managed to get the dog off my lap with a promise that we were going "bye bye," which she seemed to understand to mean something to her that made her happy. For all I knew, to her it meant a joy ride in my new car and on my lap, which see seemed to enjoy. Again, it was only temporary, so, the car would be fine, and I would wear appropriate clothing. I went into my room and started to change. Within seconds I found the dog in my room watching my every move. I wondered what was going on in her head. Was she there to make sure I wasn't leaving her behind? Was she there to hurry me along? Was she there to let me know she was there, so I wouldn't forget her? In any case, what was she doing in my room?

Since it was only for that day, it was what it was, and I got over that too. Off I went into the kitchen to grab something quick to eat out of the refrigerator and found the little one checking out it's contents with me, with her head in the refrigerator. This was getting to be interesting. Her nose was in the air sniffing everything as if she was deciding what she wanted to eat by sniffing around, while at the same time I was trying to decide what I wanted to eat by looking around. I finally decided on something. I don't even remember now what it was.

As I went to eat it, I noticed her plate was still pretty much full of the food I had given her earlier that morning. I broke off a bit of whatever I was eating and held it to her nose. She quickly but gently took the food out of my fingers and promptly ate it. As you guessed it, I shared whatever it was that I was eating and we both stood there in the kitchen sharing a special moment. All this before I was sure of finding her rightful owner that day and saying goodbye forever.

I took the makeshift leash in one hand and grabbed her under my arm and off we went on our first adventure out as man and dog, together.

6 NO SHELTER FOR THE LITTLE ONE

The shelter was not too far from where I live and even in the short ride there, as much as I was happy for the doggy that she could finally find her home, and as much as I was happy that I could finally get back to my normal life, I was feeling a little sad that this might happen within the next couple minutes. During this drive, the doggy seemed different than she was the night before when we had been in the car together for the first time. The night before she had been up on my lap and looking out the window with her tail wagging. Instead, she was on my lap, but she was lying down, not moving, and to me, she felt sad. I wondered if maybe the food had upset her stomach and if she wasn't feeling well. And then a thought turned to certainty, she was feeling what I was feeling. Sad.

My thoughts were distracted by the fact that we were arriving at the shelter. This was a shelter I was familiar with because I had seen it many times driving past it on route to and from my place. I had actually stopped in it once with a friend who was looking for a pet. I had planned to go there, but also had the address from the computer in case there were two different shelters, in which case, I would have gone to both. I parked in front of the shelter and checked the address I had gotten off the computer with the address of the shelter and they were one and the same.

But the shelter was all boarded up, in fact, it had a chain link fence around it which I hadn't recalled ever seeing. I moved closer to the front of the building and took a closer look at the signage. Sure enough, it was the shelter, or at least was, as in past tense. This was daunting to me. This shelter was on a street that I drove past, if not every day, in some cases, several times a week, and sometimes, twice a day. It seemed to me that if they had put a chain link fence around it, I would have noticed it sooner. I felt like I was in the Twilight Zone and that the fence had been put there overnight.

At the moment I realized the shelter was closed for good, there was this excitement that came over me that I couldn't explain. Knowing that I still had to try and find the dog's owner, knowing that I didn't want to have a dog, knowing that I couldn't keep a dog because of my work schedule, and many other reasons... it surprised me that I was excited the dog could stay with me, even a little longer. I was happy about it, just like unexplainably I had been happy about it the night before.

And at that moment I decided that if we were going to spend, possibly, a few more hours or even days together, there were some things that we would have to have. The doggy and I would have to go doggy shopping, and so we did.

"Doggy, you are my guest. What can I get you?" Off we went on our shopping spree of all kinds of things doggies might need and want. Here I was not even a dog owner and I was already going crazy with the toys and goodies, and all the things that I thought were silly when I watched other people buy them. They still were silly, in my mind at the time, but after all, this doggy had been through so much, a little spoiling was just what the doctor ordered, in my opinion.

I actually didn't go too far, but I did go farther than I would have expected myself to go, especially for a dog that wasn't mine and that I would not have for very much longer.

When we were shopped out, the doggy and I went home and I got to walk her up the stairs to my door with her new leash, her new dog tag, her new collar and all the trappings of a modern American spoiled dog, and some more food of course.

The rest of the afternoon was spent at Filippo's Dog Spa. That is in my bathroom, washing her, brushing her, grooming her and playing throughout it all, just doggy and me. She was given the royal treatment, and she not only was given the royal treatment, she loved it, every moment of it.

After she was all prettied up and smelled up and dolled up, I came to the realization that this little one deserved to be called something other than doggy or "you," or "Hey… you, come here." And so I named her the first name that came to mind. "Ciccina," pronounced (Chee-chee-nah).

I don't know why that name came to me as an appropriate name for her, though I knew the name well. The name comes from the Italian diminutive of the name Francesca. But why I thought it would be an appropriate name for this little one, I have no idea. Who knows? Growing up Italian-American, that name popped up in my childhood a handful of times. Come to think of it, I had a great aunt whom I never met, who lived in Italy and who was named "Ciccina." It might have come from there, but regardless of where it came from, the name suited me fine and it seemed to suit her too. She was Italian after all, she loved her pasta, and with garlic no less.

I called my Mother for the first time since I had met the doggy and told her the whole story. I then told her that I named her "Ciccina." She had a good laugh over that, but that is not the only thing she did. She went on to say, something to the effect of "Who knows for what reason this little creature is in your life and may she bring you good luck." I pretty much ignored the comment and responded by saying, "Well I'm not keeping her, and I'm working on finding her owner. I would imagine someone is really missing her." And then we hung up.

After our conversation however, her words rang in my head, as did mine. First of all, things already had been so different in that last 18 hours or so. Secondly, I had felt differently and had been hearing myself say things and do things I didn't think I would be saying or doing. And thirdly, if someone was really missing her, then why was Ciccina not really missing him or her or them and acting like she liked and knew me so well?

I started to contemplate "the meaning of life," as I liked to put it. I liked to do that every once in awhile; I thought it was good for the soul. And I had come to a couple of conclusions at that moment. The first was, that maybe Ciccina was running away and she was happy because she "manifested" me, someone who would love her as much as I had already loved her. On the other hand, if she loved her previous owner or owners, then maybe Ciccina was teaching me "the power of now." She was teaching me that in that moment, we had each other and that we could be miserable and miss someone or something, or accept that in that moment we could love who and what was in front of us, with all our being. Hmmm. That was deep.

The final conclusion was a lesson for me, and what I was getting from this was that, no matter whether she loved her owner(s) or not, she was loving what was in the now. If she hadn't loved the now, then she might have been angry from the start. And had she been angry from the start, then I might not have cared to be so kind to her. That was deep too. I wondered if I was ever with people or a situation that I wasn't happy with, or thought it should be different? I wondered how well I took it and how I made people around me feel? I knew there had been plenty of times I wasn't happy about circumstances, and I knew for a fact that I had not handled them as elegantly as Ciccina was handling this. What if I had handled myself differently in those times, would I have been loved more, cared for better, helped to my betterment? Would the circumstances have ended differently? And, for that matter, would those around me have been better off?

Had Ciccina been an ornery dog, angry about her situation, and barked or tried to bite us, we might have just had no choice but to leave her where we found her, in the street. If she had been a sulky dog, A) we wouldn't have had as much fun as we had already had together, and B) I wouldn't have joyfully gone out and bought her all these fun things for her.

So, what I was learning from Ciccina was that we really have to love what is, the way it is. We don't have to like it, but if we love it, it can be easier to change it for the better if we love it first.

All of these thoughts were good thoughts, and as much as I liked them, my "practical," thinking brain dismissed them even quicker than they came. "What do doggies know about life?" and as I dismissed my thoughts, I went on about my life. Since my day had primarily been preoccupied with Ciccina, I needed to get some work done. My work consisted of getting ready for an evening meeting that I didn't want to cancel. The evening meeting was to be with my business partner at the time, Richard and my friend Laura.

The meeting was going to be at Laura's house and I figured, Laura being a dog lover, wouldn't mind Ciccina being at our meeting. Regardless, though I knew Laura very well and knew she would be thrilled to see me with a dog, I still called her and asked her if it was okay to bring Ciccina. I also assumed that after the recent loss of Laura's two dogs, that it would actually be a good distraction for her to have Ciccina around, since I knew she was still in mourning.

However, I never thought to call Richard to see if it was okay if I brought a dog to a meeting. It never crossed my mind that it would be a problem, even though I knew Richard wasn't fond of dogs. Ciccina and I got ready to go to the meeting. I went to my bedroom closet to peruse my wardrobe to pick something to wear, and Ciccina at my feet looking inside and as well, checking out everything in there, and everything I took out of it to put on.

"Ciccina, bye, bye? Bye, bye?" Up and down Ciccina went barking and scratching at the door. "How could she have learned her name and the meaning of 'bye, bye' so quickly?" I marveled, while enjoying the excited energy in the air. She jumped so much I could hardly get her leash on and had to hold her down to finish the job. Off we went. Ciccina and I were going to our first meeting together.

7 CICCINA MEETS LAURA

When we arrived at Laura's house, Richard had already arrived and was already walking toward Laura's house gate. When Richard saw me, he waited for me at the gate before buzzing the gate to let Laura know we were there. I needed a moment to get Ciccina on her leash and gather my things. Once out of the car I started walking toward Richard with leash in hand and dog in toe. All of a sudden, Ciccina started to bark at Richard, which startled both of us. Richard was startled because he had no idea I was bringing a dog to the meeting. He knew that I wasn't that keen on having pets around and was surprised to see me with one.

I too was startled and surprised, but in my case, it was because though we hadn't met that many people together, I had never seen or heard Ciccina bark at someone like she was barking at him. I knew Richard was one of the most kind-hearted people I knew and couldn't imagine why Ciccina was acting that way. Richard was the last person that I would expect Ciccina to bark at. He also was the kind of guy that wouldn't or couldn't hurt a soul, so what would make her bark? In trying to figure it out, I got to thinking that Ciccina had a very small stature and Richard a very large stature, in fact, he is 6' 3" and that explained it for me. I thought to myself, "It's not easy being small or tall for that matter." I suppose there can be drawbacks on either side.

With Ciccina still barking at Richard, and Richard shaking his head as if to say, "What is he doing here with a dog," and I sorry that Ciccina was barking at him this way, Richard rang the gate. Laura called out, who is it, and Richard said it was he and Filippo. Upon knowing it was us, Laura buzzed the gate open.

Ciccina nearly pulled the leash from my hands with the force by which she bolted through the gate as it started opening and toward the door where Laura was standing. Once past the gate, I released the leash and let Ciccina run. And run she did, right to Laura as if she hadn't seen her for too long a time and was happy to finally see her again. Up into Laura's arms Ciccina jumped amidst excited greetings from Laura to Ciccina, "Who's this, who's this little one, who's this adorable one, who is this, huh, who...?" Along with kisses and nose butts all directed toward Ciccina, it seemed like Laura practically forgot all about us as Richard and I approached.

"She's so cute?" Laura exclaimed to me when I finally reached her and she put Ciccina down and hugged me. "I love her." "I can't imagine you with a dog, it's so funny to me," she went on to say. She hugged Richard as well, and we all were beckoned into the house while the love fest between Ciccina and Laura continued.

Laura guided us to her dining room table and asked us to make ourselves comfortable and left the room. Of course, Ciccina followed her. "Whatcha doin', huh whatcha doin'?" I could hear from the dining room that Ciccina and she were having quite a conversation and getting to know each other.

All the while I heard dish sounds and water running and who knows what else was going on in the kitchen as Richard and I spread our paperwork out getting ready for our meeting. "Yesh, this is for you sweetheart, yesh it is, I thought you'd like it... and here's your water..." I heard Laura say in a baby talk kind of way. All this time, I thought Laura had been preparing some snacks for us, as she usually did when I visited. Being that her Mother was Italian, Laura got the part of feeding her guests down. And indeed she had, only the guest of honor that night was Ciccina.

When Laura finally came and sat down, she told me, "You have to tell me her whole story, I just love her." I couldn't have been happier to tell Ciccina's story, short though it was at that point; I was becoming very fond of the story, and Ciccina. That wasn't the time to get into my whole effort in finding her a home and the plan of action I had taken, and the couple involved, etc. But I told Laura this much. I told her that when I first saw her in the street, that I heard myself say, "come to me," and that the moment I questioned that thought with a "what would I do with her?" the answer came clearly, "bring her to Laura." For some reason, and for whatever that was worth, I felt that I had to tell her that.

Laura heard what I said, looked at me, and said, "Honey I love her, I would take her in a minute, but she's not my dog. I can usually tell when a dog is my dog." As if right on cue, Ciccina jumps onto Laura's lap and starts to kiss/lick her face. "You know we are talking about you don't you, yesh, yesh, you love giving little doggy kisses don't you?", Laura gushed with joy.

"What are you calling her?" she turned her head to ask me while she was being lapped up one side of her face and down the other. "Ciccina," I responded. "Ciccina?" she questioned. "That's cute, but it's not her name," she replied. "I know," I said, "but I had to call her something, and besides, it's only temporary. Now let's get to work."

"Okay Cic, Cic, what is it again?" Laura asked, having trouble remembering how to say her name. "Ciccina," I reminded her. "Ciccina? Okay, Ciccina, we gotta work now, so go play with the toys I gave you, run along." She even gave her toys? Then down to business we got.

During our meeting, every time Laura would get up for coffee or water or something, Ciccina would be right at her heels and we would hear all the sweet names and phrases one could think of coming from the kitchen or the hall or the living room, all directed at Ciccina. Wherever Laura was Ciccina was, as were the sounds of bonding.

At one point we heard the front door open, which could only mean one thing, Laura's husband Bob was home. Ciccina, the newly, self-proclaimed protector of us all, and protector of Laura's house, barked and ran to the front door. As she arrived at the door, the barking immediately stopped and the sounds were of her wagging as distinguished by the clicking sound her collar made by hitting up against her tag.

I could just tell from the sounds, that she had started bouncing up and down. This baffled me. Bob was a man that Ciccina did not know and he also was tall. Bob was, in fact, as tall as Richard, and yet, Ciccina wasn't barking at him. There went my theory about being of small stature and barking at someone of large stature.

I didn't have time to ponder on that because Bob walked in with Ciccina in his arms and her licking his face like crazy. I was thinking to myself, "This dog really belongs here, these are dog people who let themselves have their faces licked and everything. Ciccina has so much love to give and so much licking she wants to do; she really deserves to be able to lick to her heart's content."

Bob interrupted my thought process with "Whose dog is this?" "Filippo's," Laura immediately answered. "No, it's not my dog, I just rescued it and am keeping her until we find her owner," I retorted. "Well, it looks to me like she found her home. You're going to have a tough time getting rid of this one," Laura insisted.

What would make her say that? I thought it was an interesting comment for her to make. And before I had time to reflect on that, she made yet another comment that was just as thought provoking. "That's interesting," she says as Bob walks away from the dining room to let us continue our work, "Bob is not a little dog person, but I can tell, he likes her." "Maybe she IS your dog then?" I said. "Honey, really, with what I have just been through with the loss of Nicky and Andy, I couldn't even think of another dog. But if I was sure it was my dog, I would take her off your hands right now."

Our meeting eventually came to an end, after which, I had to pry Laura and Ciccina apart so I could take Ciccina home. Bob came into the dining room to say his goodbyes as well. I had the feeling he did so more to say goodbye to Ciccina than Richard and I. Nonetheless, we all said our goodbyes and we all went our separate ways, every one of them without dogs, and me with Ciccina.

On the way home I went back to pondering why Ciccina barked at Richard like crazy and bounced up and down for Bob, both strangers to her and both very tall men. And then it hit me. Richard does not like dogs. He wouldn't mistreat one, but he would just rather they stayed away from him. Could Ciccina have picked that up? If so, how?

Earlier in the day I was dismissing the possibility that this dog, or any dog, for that matter, could know anything about the mysteries of life, so to speak. I had thought that she couldn't possibly know that we have to "be in the now" in order to live our lives in the best possible way. And at that point, she may have been sniffing out, sensing, or "knowing," who was a dog lover and who was not. Was I able to do that? Was I supposed to be able to do that?

Though it had been a long day already, the evening was still young and I had plenty of questions that my new friend Ciccina had raised for me. And being a seeker of answers I wanted answers. That made me think of a lady, Dorothy, that a friend of mine, Marco, had introduced me to, only months before. Introduce isn't quite the word for it, actually. When Marco met Dorothy, he immediately called me and told me that there was a lady in San Diego I had to meet. He told me how she was a Healer and a Spiritual Advisor and that I needed to meet her. He then repeated that I had to meet her.

I agreed to meet her, and he continued to insist that I really had to meet her soon. At that point, Marco and I had been really good friends for a long time. I knew him really well, but I had never heard him like that before. I really didn't know what he wanted me to do. I finally asked him, "Are you saying I should get in my car and drive from Los Angeles to San Diego right now to meet her?" "No," he said, "but you have to meet her soon."

Well, a week or so later, Marco arranged for Dorothy and I to meet in Los Angeles. And when I finally met her, I found out I already knew her, even though I had never actually met her or knew of her. I just knew her. Marco too lived on a busy street. The day

Dorothy was supposed to arrive to meet me at his place, I was standing outside his place doing something or other, when a car went by. I knew that Dorothy was in that car. Minutes later, Marco came out to join me and I told him that Dorothy had arrived. He looked at his watch and told me that she wasn't due for a couple hours or so.

He asked me, "How would you know, anyway?" I said, "I don't know, a car went by and I just knew it was Dorothy. She was in the car with another woman." Marco answered," Ah, well then it's definitely not her, she's coming by herself."

A couple minutes after that conversation two women walk down the sidewalk and I turned to Marco and said, "See, I told you Dorothy was here." "You're right," Marco said with delight, "How did you know that?" "I don't know," I responded, more surprised than he was.

Sure enough Dorothy had arrived with her daughter Tricia. Unbeknownst to me, later that day Marco and I learned that while driving past Marco's place, Tricia had asked her Mother, when she saw, "Is that Marco?" "No," answered Dorothy, "that's Filippo." "How do you know?" asked Tricia, knowing that she had never met me before. "Because I know!" answered Dorothy assured of her knowing.

None of us, knew each other's last name at that point, so there was no looking each other up on the computer or anything like that. It was admittedly weird for me. But it was amazingly beautiful. We had a wonderful day together, with Dorothy teaching us, and others who eventually came to meet her as well, so many things. As tired as I was and my brain filled with so much information, or rather, my mind blown with the kind of information she shared, it was still a day I didn't want to end.

Once she went back home, I began the many phone calls to Dorothy in San Diego with question after question after question. Almost every time I called Dorothy, she would laugh or chuckle for reasons unbeknownst to me during our conversation. I would be puzzled each time this happened, at first. Each time it happened I would ask her why she was laughing, and she would say something like, "they told me you would ask me that?" "They?" "Who are they?" I would ask, perplexed. "The guides," she would answer. "In fact, remember when I told you..." and she would go on to remind me that she had started to answer my question back when I didn't even know I had that specific question, and on the conversation would go as would my learning.

As I learned more about Dorothy, I came to learn she is a special kind of Spiritual Advisor. She calls herself an Energetic Alchemist and says that her mission is to awaken, accelerate and activate people's gifts. Much like so many other things that we talked about, I didn't know what this meant, but everything she said intrigued me. Though I didn't understand everything we talked about, nor was I convinced that I believed in "Guides" or what have you, everything she said resonated with me. Even though my mind wasn't getting it, within my body, it just felt right. I wasn't used to thinking about what felt right, "in my body," or not, but talking to her gave me a sensation that it was "right," in my body.

In retrospect, it was just my mind that was having the most trouble with everything, and though it got in the way sometimes, I also was trying to find a way to make both my mind and my body feel "right." In other words, I wanted to find the science behind some of what she was saying to allow my engineering mind to connect the dots, so to speak.

Tonight, after my meeting with Richard and Laura and the ideas that came up thanks to Ciccina, I was ripe for one of these mind-blowing conversations and Dorothy was just the person I was looking forward to having it with. When I got home, I settled on my couch, with Ciccina under my arms... (Hmm, how things had changed), and I settled in for a long phone conversation. I had questions, I wanted answered and I knew Dorothy had them.

I was delighted Dorothy was home and answered the phone. She sounded happy to hear from me, and after a few pleasantries, she said, "So tell me what happened." "What happened?" I questioned. "Yes, you called me to tell me what happened, so tell me," she answered matter-of-factly. "Well, I found a dog yesterday," I hesitatingly answered.

"And?" she asked. "And what?" I retorted. "Come on Filippo, I know something big is going on and it has you perplexed, but understand that it's all part of the process of your awakening and you just have to breathe and experience it," she replied.

"What?" I said. "Nothing big, I just found a dog, that's all," I continued. "I'm gonna find its owner and that will be that," I said. "Right, okay," she quipped back. "What? What are you talking about, what did I say? I just said I found a dog, so what's the big deal, I'm gonna find its owner and that will be that," I insisted.

"Okay, Filippo, you called me, remember?" she reminded me.

"I was just, I was just wondering how animals know things sometimes when we don't," I finally asked her. Funny to me in retrospect that I was asking Dorothy how animals know things "when sometimes we don't," when clearly Dorothy knew something that I didn't, and I was asking her how animals know, as opposed to how she knew.

But Dorothy's answer included all that. "Animals can connect, just like we all can to the source of all-knowing and they use their senses in ways we can, but that most humans don't," she said.

"Dorothy," I said.

"Yes, Filippo," she answered.

"I think there's something going on that is really weird. My Mother said today that she hopes this dog brings something special into my life and that she wishes me luck, or something like that, or that it brings me luck. Then tonight, my friend Laura said that I would have a hard time getting rid of her. It's funny they should say that. I feel this strong connection to this dog. It's weird isn't it?" I asked of her.

She goes on to say, "No Filippo, it's not weird, it's perfect. You have been asking to be awakened and accelerated and activated.

You and I have been working on the higher dimensions together since before we met in this dimension. You have such an understanding of whom you are and what you have come to be and do, in the other dimensions, you just need to bring that understanding into this dimension. This dog is here to teach you a lot. This is your dog until you learn what you need to learn and then once you've learned it, and only then, will you find her a home." I was quiet. "Filippo, are you there?" she asked.

"Yes, Dorothy," I answered.

"It's going to be alright honey. In fact, it's going to be better than all right. You just have to trust. All is in divine right order and timing. You just have to breathe." And with that she said, "I gotta go to bed, good night honey and give my best to, what's her name?" "Ciccina," I answered. "What?" she asked.

"Ciccina," I repeated.

"Okay," she says, "give my best to her. Good night."

I said, "Good night," and as I hung up the phone, I thought that I had heard and done enough for one day. A good night was indeed in order, for me and for, "what's her name," and to bed we went.

8 DAY TWO, DAY THREE, DAY FOUR... AND ALL IS WELL

The morning of day two began much like the morning of day one. I was excited to get up and open the office door to greet an equally excited doggy anxious to greet me. This time, however, a lot had changed, me, for one, in a few particular ways, and I would like to think, her too. But looking back, she always knew who she was, and it seems, where she was. It was me who was learning who she was, who she was in my life, and in many respects, whom I was, or whom I was going to be, or something like that.

What also had changed was that doggy woke up with a name; Ciccina, and I called her by name, to which she seemed to respond. Something else that had changed, instead of a makeshift leash and collar, we had the real thing. I put the leash on her, and off we went on what already seemed like our routine morning walk together.

Upon our return, I prepared her breakfast and served it to her on my china bowls, no less. It's curious to me, looking back, how I bought Ciccina many dog accessories, and could have easily and cheaply bought her a bowl, but for some reason, at that point, I had not. And for some reason, I was happy to serve her in my own bowls. Was it because I figured it was something I could manage without, whereas the collar and the leash were more necessary? Maybe, or maybe not, because when I thought about it, the toys and other things we could have done without also, so there went that theory.

I guess I just decided that nothing was too good for my Ciccina, even if she was only my temporary dog. In actuality, what I ended up doing was relegating a whole set of dishes to Ciccina, at least for the time being.

Having finally gone to the health food store the day before, I had bought some food for her that I was happy with, food without things in it that I thought doggies shouldn't have to eat, and fed her the first batch. I was thrilled to see she liked it. This day was starting out great.

It didn't bother me feeding her my food, during the day or at night, but for breakfast I didn't think our eating habits were that compatible. Besides I wanted to make sure she was getting her vitamins and minerals. At the time, I ate like a vegan, no meat, no fish, no eggs, no dairy. I am not so sure that dogs are meant to be vegans. So, I wanted to make sure she got her fill of all the meat she needed, if in fact she needed meat.

After my own breakfast, I returned to the phone to call my new friends, the couple I met a couple evenings before, to ask them if they had any luck in finding the owner(s) of the dog. When I didn't get an answer I left a message and returned to Craig's List, and anything else I could think of to find Ciccina her rightful owner(s), and her "rightful" name, for that matter.

Little did I know that this would become my routine for several more days and that it would be to no avail. Soon I stopped receiving returned calls from the couple and soon, looking at Craig's list etc., got old. More than getting old, I was starting to believe the feeling inside of me that Ciccina wasn't supposed to be going back the way she came.

In those days after rescuing/meeting Ciccina, I had had to visit several people for business purposes and make some social calls. On every single visit I would have people surprised that not only did I have a dog, but also that I wasn't leaving the dog at home and attending to my business on my own. In short order I had become one of those people who brought their dogs with them to meetings and everywhere else.

But, I did always call before a meeting at someone's home or office and ask them if they would mind my bringing Ciccina along with me. Invariably they would say that I could bring her, which would please me.

I never stopped to ask myself if they were just being nice, like I was just being nice, back in the days before Ciccina, or wondered if they were unable to say "no," like I had a hard time saying "no" to my friends' and their dogs. It even got to the point that I was taking her to restaurant lunch meetings if there were locations that accepted dogs and had outside patios. I even found myself scoping out restaurants and cafes that allowed dogs.

What had become of me, and what had become of my life? I wasn't recognizing either one.

On one of my many visits with my friend Marco, at his place, I had brought "my" dog, Ciccina, as per usual. During this particular visit, Marco had a young lady friend visit him, unannounced. At a certain point, Marco and I got into a conversation about something, and the young lady started conversing with Ciccina. When she was done "talking" with Ciccina, she joined us and told us that Ciccina was really happy to be with me. I looked at her with surprise, disbelief and much curiosity.

"What do you mean?" I asked her, "How can you tell?"

"I can talk to dogs, and that's what I was doing down there on the floor while you guys were talking," she informed us mater of factly. Evidently, she was a sort of animal whisperer and a medium, and she had taken it upon herself to communicate with Ciccina. She knew nothing of the circumstances of how I came upon Ciccina, only that I had recently rescued her.

She went on to say that Ciccina did not want to go back to her old owner. She said the owner was a lady who possibly had Alzheimer's and that she was neglectful of the dog and forgot to feed her and walk her. She said Ciccina knew what she was doing when she ventured away that night we met.

I didn't know what to think at that point. Marco quickly chimed in and said, "I told you this is your dog," and leaned back and had himself a good laugh. He had said this to me over the phone and then again as soon as he met her and saw her and I together the first time. I quickly retorted to him and everyone else who would say that, and a lot of people did, that, "No she's not, and it's only temporary!"

"Right!" they would say, "you keep believing that, you'll see." "I'll see what? This is not my dog!" I couldn't speak more plainly than that and I couldn't have been more sure, in my mind.

9 REALITY CHECK

Reality started to sink in that I have a dog, and this dog has me. I had given up on the hopes that we, or I, at this point, would find Ciccina's owner. Whether the owner really was someone with Alzheimer's or not, I had done everything I knew to do to find him or her. I also knew in my heart, that which was obvious to everyone else, and was becoming obvious to me, I wasn't supposed to find her owner. If I truly lived in the moment, then in the moment, I was her owner, and this was my dog.

Having eventually accepted this, I changed my approach. Instead of the task of finding her old owner, I now charged myself with the task of finding her new owner. There were two things I became sure of, in the moment, her owner was me, and in the future, it wouldn't and couldn't be me.

Mind you, I still had to work, and I still did of course, only work was a little different. Since I worked at home, I would do my work as per usual, except I would be doing the work at my desk with Ciccina on my lap, more often than not. Ciccina would come with me to meetings more often then not. Ciccina would be the center of attention more often than not. And none of this bothered me. Truth be told, I enjoyed it.

I had often wondered why people rushed home to be with their dogs or cats. I had often wondered why people would bring their

47

dogs and leave them in the car as opposed to leaving them at home. I had often wondered why people took animals to stores, events, meetings, and people's houses.

Well, I wondered no more.

Ciccina didn't just come with me to my friends' houses or to meetings, she would come with me to yoga, the gym, the store, and to so much more. Of course she wasn't always welcome, but she seemed happy enough waiting for me in my car, rather than on the rare occasion when she would be waiting at home. Or maybe it was me that was happier, or both?

I remember once taking her out of the car for a walk after a yoga class. The yoga instructor, who was a friend of mine, came out of the yoga studio, and upon seeing her, said "I didn't know you had a dog." "I don't," I was still saying. "We have each other until we find her a new home and a rightful new owner," I said to him.

He then took a walk with us around the block a couple times and we talked as we walked and watched Ciccina run after the birds, smell everything she could smell, etc. At a certain point my friend interrupts our conversation to say to me, "She IS so your dog!"

I just turned to face him, smiled, shook my head in mild disagreement and went right back to our conversation. I had given up on fighting it. But I hadn't given up on finding her a good home. It had to be a good home, not just any home, it's not what I would have wanted for her before, and certainly not now. So I wasn't going to put her up for adoption in the paper or on the Internet. I was going to use my network of friends to find her the best home I could.

I started my search with my a phone call to my own Mother. She said no, but she said she wanted to meet Ciccina before I gave her away to someone. That was not like my Mother. It wasn't that she wanted to see if she liked Ciccina before deciding. It was simply the fact that she felt Ciccina was significant to me, and she wanted to meet her, even though she knew I wouldn't be having her for long.

I then called one of my brothers, who also said no, but that he wanted to meet her too and have his kids meet her, before I gave her away, which I thought was also interesting.

I called my other brother and he said the exact same thing. Why did everybody want to meet Ciccina? And what was I supposed to do, take her on a farewell tour of my family? My family members did not live near one another. How would they all get to meet Ciccina, and how long would it be before we all got around to seeing each other?

In a subsequent conversation with my Mother, I was recounting to her the fact that both my brothers wanted to meet Ciccina. She told me that that one of my brothers was going to be visiting her in a month or so. My Mother asked me why couldn't I keep her until at least then, so Ciccina and I could visit, and they could meet her.

I couldn't imagine, at the time, keeping Ciccina a month or so, just so my Mother and brother could meet her. Around the same time, my other brother called me saying that he and his wife had been talking about Ciccina and might want to reconsider taking her if she was good with kids. They told me the same thing my Mother had told me, that they would be visiting my Mother in a month or so, and asked if I could just hold on to her until then.

With the prospect of a good home for Ciccina and a great dog for my nieces, I felt it important enough, and such a great potential opportunity for everyone all around, that I should stop my search and keep Ciccina with me until I visited my Mother.

I had at that point committed myself to what felt like long-term, at least a month more with Ciccina. At this point, when people would ask me what my plans were for Ciccina, I would tell them, I was bringing her home to meet Mother. "So it's serious?" they would quip. "Very," I would respond. We would laugh, and of course, it was funny and all true.

I felt that there was a potential here that once someone in my family met Ciccina, that someone would want her for their own.

49

And just the thought of that possibility made me happy for all of them, including Ciccina and me.

I felt assured that we had found her a home and all I had to do is just wait it out, or as my friend Dorothy would say, "breathe."

10 ANOTHER DAY... ANOTHER LESSON

As the days went by, Ciccina and I bonded more and more. With the pressure removed from my having to find her a home, I could enjoy her a little more than I felt I could before.

As the days went by, we started getting to know each other's idiosyncrasies. I don't know what she thought of mine, but I found most of hers to be either funny or interesting. Whether her idiosyncrasies were funny or interesting to me, I started to recognize them as perfect. That is, perfect for a dog, and for that matter, maybe even more perfect than some of the things I was doing for myself as a human.

In actuality, I was really learning to be in the "now" more and more, and to be present in each moment. I also was trying to "connect" more and more. One of the things I started doing that was different for me was trying my hand at seeing if I could tell who was a dog lover and who wasn't. Not that that was so important to me, but I figured, if I could learn to do that alongside Ciccina, maybe I could then apply that skill to other things. In fact, I started to apply it to other areas of my life, like, "Is this person a people lover or not?" "Is this person a friendly person or not?" "Does this person love himself/herself?" I was trying to get a "vibe," figuring that this was what Ciccina was doing. I suppose some would call it using a sixth sense.

And speaking of senses, I was learning that in everything Ciccina did, she used them, senses. The sixth sense was the one that had me intrigued the most, up until then. Among some of my friends who dabbled in the esoteric energies, let's call them, they were fascinated with her "sixth" sense and the extent to which she seemed to be in tune. At times it seemed to them, and to me, that she somehow manipulated situations that weren't the way they were supposed to be until Ciccina literally stepped into the room. Two of these friends both even took it as far as asking the question, "I wonder how she knew it was supposed to be you?" It's truly as if she knew. One could argue that it was all a coincidence, but one would probably, easily lose the argument.

One could also more successfully argue that maybe I was "connecting" too, because after having been to a gala event, where there was food, what would make me feel the need to have munchies? What would make me drive home after a long day and before getting out of the car, pull out of the garage again and drive to the store? Surely I had something in the house, if nothing else, I obviously had pasta, since I made it for myself later that evening. Actually, correction, I made it for myself, but Ciccina ate it. Nevertheless, there was pasta and who knows what else, but I still went out for food, or at least, I thought that was why I was going out.

I have seen many a stray dog in my lifetime, what would have made me stop and eye this one? And when I say eye, at one point, across a busy street, in the dark, our eyes literally met. Was I using this "sixth" sense also, already, and didn't really know it? Was I feeling like I needed to go out that night because I sensed that I was supposed to meet someone, something at a certain time, and interpreted it as hunger for munchies? I was getting beyond my comprehension of the possibilities as I had seen them at that point and quickly dismissed it all as a bit too woo, woo for me.

But sixth sense aside, what about the other senses? Was I using my other five senses effectively, often enough, appropriately, etc.? Was I aware when I was using them? Was I using what I gained from the sensing to make better, more informed decisions in my life, or at the very least, to just have a better experience of life?

These were questions that started coming up the more time I spent with Ciccina, especially during our walk time. I hadn't recalled having these questions come up before. I went with the moment and allowed the questions to come, as if I didn't have enough questions, and hoped the answers would follow.

For example, I started to notice how Ciccina used her nose a lot. This is obvious to everyone who has even see a dog, not even having had to be the caretaker of one. But Ciccina was using her nose not just to smell, but also to "feel" things out. She would distinguish textures from just the touch of her nose, or so it seemed to me.

She not only touched with her nose, but also touched with her paws, touching things, just for the sake of touching them, to "feel" them out, at least, again, it seemed so to me.

I started watching her more and more on our walks and started to reflect more and more on the meaning behind the otherwise "senseless" things she did. Sure, there were times that I thought some things she did were just taking up too much time. There were times I would feel annoyed and felt like what I had to do was more important than what she had to do. But when I was able to take the time, I felt that there was something for me in everything that she was doing.

At first, I thought "going out for her to do her business," was just so she could do her business, and then we could go back to doing what we were doing, or at least I could. But doing her "business" was only part of it, every walk was an experience to her, and "serious business."

Who knows, maybe this was her business? And if we went along with that idea, then what kind of "Business" was she in? For that matter, what kind of "Business" was I in? She got me questioning myself. As for her, I started to figure out that Ciccina was in the business of "being," or, of "living," if you will. And me? I was in the singing business, or the radio business, or the... you name the business, and it was everything and anything but "being," or "living," as I was experiencing it. "Being" and "living" never factored into my mind when it came to what kind of business I was in, or what it was that I "did for a living," even though I was one of the few people who I knew who was actually doing something they loved for "work," thinking of it like I was doing now was beyond my understanding; but I knew enough to know it needed exploring.

As I watched, it became funny to me how Ciccina acted, and was, so to speak, the Capitan of her ship during our/her walks. For that matter, she seemed like she was always in command. Her size and stature and the fact that I was "taking care of her," started to seem to me more like I was serving her.

More and more during our walks, I "let" her do her "frivolous" things, and I just watched her. I was learning something, but I wasn't quite sure just what that something was. And I watched her more and more intently. On the one hand, I was getting caught up in the moment of "being in the moment" with her. On the other hand, this was our moment, in the sense that soon she would most likely be with members of my family and we wouldn't be spending as much time together. So it was now or never.

I was paying attention. In a sense I was living a dog's life vicariously through her. It seemed like my life was on hold while I watched her. At first I thought I was the one in control of this little doggy, guiding her around on my leash, letting her out, for the most part only when it was convenient for me; pulling her back toward the house when I had had enough, and after she had finally done her "business...."

In time, it seemed like it took her longer and longer to do her "business," the "business" I originally thought we had gone out to do. Had Ciccina figured out that after doing that, she would be usually ushered back toward home? Had she started holding her "business," until she had enough of the other "business" at hand, making me wait on her to get it all in, before "getting it all out?"

If she were doing this, I wouldn't blame her one bit. In those few minutes, twice a day "out in the world," was she "living?" In fact, in those few minutes, to me, it seemed like she was "living" more than I lived during my twenty-four hours "in my world." That was a big statement. Where did that come from? Who says things like that? What was I thinking? What was going on? I was just walking a little dog that I didn't want pooping in my house. Why does this simple task have to raise so many questions? What kind of questions were these, where were they coming from, and why? And why now?

Whether on our walks around the block, or to the car and back, to and from a meeting or the store or wherever, more and more I watched her. I watched her "Be," I watched her "Live."

What kind of questions are these, I wondered? Where were they coming from? More importantly, what are the answers? How will they, or might they serve me if and/or when I get them? I would ponder and ponder, and occasionally I would tell my friends what I was thinking. They all thought it was strange, as did I, frankly.

Millions of people had cared for dogs the world over for Centuries. Rarely did I hear people talk about their dogs like they were metaphysical teachers or some kind of guru. Maybe it was because I knew we only had a short time together and I wanted to experience as much of Ciccina as I could while we were together? Maybe it was because I had been seeking greater metaphysical understanding of my life, my experience, my mission and my existence on this planet that it was all coming to a head? Maybe having such a big life "disruptor," as this dog coming into my life and taking me out of my comfort zone and pattern, opened up other things and possibilities? Who knows?

Luckily, I did have a few friends that recognized that I was in the middle of some sort of transition, or should I say, transformation, and Dorothy in particular, was a big help during this part, sometimes. I say "sometimes," because, sometimes, she would just tell me to "breathe. And then she would say, "It is all happening." And this did not seem like a help to me at all, though I know now that it was a bigger help than giving me answers I was still not ready to hear, or learn or that I needed, and perhaps wanted to discover on my own.

Still, over all, things had gotten a bit confusing, and in many ways, I let them. So much of my life had changed. I noticed the attention I got was different too, because I was with Ciccina. I noticed how people reacted to her and how people smiled when they saw her. Complete strangers would stop to talk because I was walking her, or she me, whatever. Sometimes, people would start out saying things to Ciccina and then end up talking with me.

A lot of people say pets are icebreakers. People like to stop to pet a dog, or admire it. I liked it too. I liked people admiring Ciccina and saying she was cute. I also liked people acknowledging me. I got to thinking how I had lived in my neighborhood for many years. I enjoy walking, and had been walking around my block, or to the post office, or the grocery store, or just walking around for years. I had gotten more people saying hello to me because I had Ciccina than all my hours of walking in all those years put together.

Did we really need a dog to break the ice? I'm very much a people person; I like people and generally, people like me. But when we cross each other on a sidewalk, are we not able to "sniff" each other out, and recognize, "Here comes a people person, I think I'll say hi?" I used to say "Hi," more often, but I had stopped, without realizing I had.

People, what has happened to us?

What has happened to me?

And was Ciccina really having more of a life than I?

11 COMING TO MY "SENSES"

As if my world didn't seem to be topsy-turvy enough, I had started contemplating not just the meaning of my life, but also the meaning of my dog's life. And she wasn't even my dog.

On the one hand, to some, it had seemed like I had lost my senses, for this dog, and to others, that I had lost my senses because of this dog. The interesting thing was, that while seemingly losing my senses, I was actually connecting more than ever with my five senses, and amazingly, my sixth sense as well. It started to happen subtly at first, and I almost didn't notice it, but little by little I was sure it was happening or at least conscious of it.

For example, in watching Ciccina walk day in and day out, I noted her stopping to smell this or touch that. At times, Ciccina would stop to listen to this, or bark at that, and all the while what was I doing, I was watching her "be" and "live."

I remember as a child I used to touch things just for the sake of touching and feeling. I remember also being told over and over again, "Don't touch." When I learned to read, it seemed every store had a sign that read, "PLEASE DON'T TOUCH." I thought they had written that sign just for me, because it just so happened to be directly in front of all the things I would have wanted to touch.

At the same time as a child I had this "trait," that almost every breakable thing I touched, I would break. The desire to touch and this "trait" were a terrible combination. It wasn't as if I did it on purpose, but I often dropped things as a child by accident or negligence or grabbed them too firmly, which lead to breakage. Either it was one or both of those, or I touched more things than the average child, in which case it might have actually been proportionate.

I also was very picky about the things I touched. I liked to touch real things, and remember being able to tell the difference with my touch if something was real or not, when the eyes were deceiving me. As a small child, I had toys, and things that I could play with, and that were indestructible, but most of them were made out of plastic.

The stuff that I wanted to touch most was not made of plastic, it was "real" stuff. What was "real" to me? I used to like the touch of things like cotton, wood, crystal, stones, precious metals, silver, gold, and such. I used to think of that stuff as alive, having energy, though I didn't know what that was at the time, nor did I use that term. It just made me feel good to touch something real, especially if it was made into something that I thought was pretty, clever, artistic or creative.

I remember walking through churches and liking the feel of marble columns, walking through stores and feeling the material on the clothes, and walking past plants and feeling the leaves and getting a sensation from it. I also remember the sensation when I would touch what I thought was a marble column, and then remove my hand quickly, because it was stucco. Similarly, I could tell if an item of clothing hanging on a rack in a store was made out of a synthetic fiber or a natural fiber, and usually I knew specifically what natural fiber.

I used to say, "I don't want to play with my toys, I want to play with this." "Don't touch it," would be the usual response to almost everything I was referring to as "this." Of course, as an adult I understand now, some of the stuff, glass etc., would have hurt me and others, had I broken them. Besides the things I liked to play with, cost more than my toys and were made to be decorative, or functionally beautiful.

Growing up, I noticed that I seemed to be the only one with this fascination of touching, among other things. I also noticed that in school, how things felt, and much less how we felt about things, was not a focus. I was being focused to think rather than feel. And though I wasn't sure of the subtle difference at the time, the end result was what I had become. I had became a person who thought a lot about a lot of things. Though the "thinking" a lot was in my nature, thinking more was rewarded, and I got the idea that "feeling," wasn't.

If you ask me, if I had lost my "senses," I had lost them long time ago.

I came to believe I had somehow thrown out the baby with the bath water. I didn't keep my sense of curiosity as to how something would feel, or better yet, I didn't keep that feeling of getting energy, or whatever I thought it was, from touching something that was "real," and at one time, possibly alive, or still alive, for that matter.

I had lost my sense of touch. Obviously, I touched my computer keyboard, and my fork and spoon, and paperwork, and pens, etc. But touching something for the sake of touching and feeling with my hands for the sense of feeling was not part of my life. And all those things I touched were not "real" to me anyway. All of a sudden, thanks to Ciccina and these questions and answers, I wanted so much to have that as part of my life again. Ciccina was using her sense of touch; I wanted to use mine also.

As time passed, as I walked with Ciccina, more and more, I would touch. I would touch a tree trunk when we passed by a tree, I would touch the dirt when she stopped to smell something. I would brush my hands across grass or a bush, just to feel it go across my fingers and hand, because I could, and because evidently, "living" my life depended on it.

When at home, I had taken up more the practice of touching there too, and would touch and feel more things around my house. Or better yet, I would touch the things I touched everyday, like plates, glasses, towels, silk pillows, etc., only I would touch them for the sake of touching them and sensing what I felt. I would see if I could sense anything, feel anything that I hadn't felt before, and sometimes I would, and sometimes I wouldn't.

Even when I wouldn't "sense" something, touching was fun again, and I had discovered it again. And possibly there was a higher awareness of my sense of touch, than I ever had before, thanks to Ciccina.

But I didn't stop there; I was ready to tackle more of my senses, in fact, I wanted to awaken all of them. I was even more certain after my new found and new born experience with touch, that my living life depended on my senses being reawakened, and possibly in some cases awakened for the first time. I watched and learned, and as Ciccina would stop, the next thing she did which I focused on was that she smelled things. When she would stop to smell something, I would take the opportunity to stop and smell something too.

I didn't know how to consciously, randomly smell, like she seemed to. On occasion we smell a bad odor, like from a toilet or gas station or something, and we may remark on it with disgust and move on. On other occasions we smell a good odor, like food cooking in a kitchen, coffee brewing or bread toasting, and we get hungry and look forward to eating. But when was the last time any of us stopped just to smell the air on any given day, for the sake of smelling?

Could we walk out of our homes and offices and take a big whiff and distinguish the difference in one day's air scent versus another day's air scent? What if we could? What could we learn from it, what would it tell us?

At first, it seemed weird to me to just stop and smell, so I had to stop and smell something, like a rose or a flower, but after a while I got comfortable enough to just stop and take a good whiff, of air, wherever I was when Ciccina stopped. After I did it a few times, it didn't feel as weird, and before long I started picking up a scent.

In our society, traditionally, maybe women are more in touch with that sense of smell then men, but so much of what we smell is manufactured, synthetic, in other words, not real. It doesn't excite us, our senses, or our brains, like "real" scents do.

Candles, perfumes, sprays and bathroom deodorizers, most of them are not "real." Heck, we hardly get to enjoy the fresh smell of home cooked food anymore. We want a cookie; we buy a cookie, for the most part, already made in the store. No smell. Sure, if you stopped to smell a cookie, you might pick up a scent.

Back in the day when I was growing up and my Mom would be making cookies, I remember like it was yesterday, I could smell those cookies baking from any room in the house. The sense of smell would be excited and and so would I. Like Ciccina, when I would open a can of food for her, sure, it wasn't the same, but she would start to smell the air, taking in as much of the smell as she could, long before the food would go into her bowl and long before she ate it.

Something happens when we smell and it goes with the whole enjoyment and pleasure of a thing. Like a cookie, I'd smell the cookies in the oven and my mouth would start to salivate just from the smell. When the cookies were done and I was allowed to have one fresh out of the oven I could touch the freshness and the sense of touch would be excited. On occasion they would still be too hot, and depending on the cookie, sometimes very moist and my sense of sight was excited to see the chocolate melt, as hot chocolate chips in cookies would, for example.

Then finally the moment would arrive when I could put the cookie in my mouth and chew it, feel the texture and taste it in my mouth. My senses not only were excited individually but they all worked together for a literal full body experience. I have heard women describe that very experience, with chocolate, especially, as "orgasmic." I wonder if many of us are having enough "orgasmic" experiences when it comes to food or the experiences of our senses working together.

If Mom had baked the cookies, as in my particular example above, there would also be a "Mom loves me" dimension to the experience, which excites the sixth sense, I imagine and kicks it all up a notch.

As important as I was learning that pleasure was, and how little of it I had in my life, it was not only about pleasure. The more I got to thinking about these questions the deeper I went. I was putting two and two together and I was discovering things that maybe I already knew and maybe we all knew, but many of us, certainly me, had lost touch with. In the case of the sense of smell, smelling the cookie also starts the digestive process. It is all connected. When we eat food that we didn't smell first, or in some cases didn't "see," as in the case of food our body doesn't recognize as food, the digestive process is out of sync. No wonder I was having so many digestive problems as an adult.

In my further research I came to learn that there is a whole science and research around artificial colors and "food" additives, to make the body "think" it is eating "real" food. Though it is a science, it is not what I as a child would have considered "real," and evidently my body wasn't exactly being fooled. Only, I didn't know this.

Much like having been disconnected with my sense of touch, I had lost connection with my sense of smell. Though I cooked for myself often and though I ate as healthy as I knew how, I had not connected the importance of the sense of touch and smell to my eating experience. For that matter, I had disconnected from touch and smell, in many ways with my living, or not so, "living" experience. Somehow I knew that my life wasn't "real," but I didn't know how to get back to "real." I couldn't imagine that it would be by way of a dog, or my sense of touch or smell, for that matter, but I was willing to try it.

Back to the sense of smell, I am sure I could research the scientific, biological and evolutional importance of smelling, but Ciccina didn't read books or look things up on the Internet, she just did what came naturally. She smelled.

In exercising my sense of smell right along with Ciccina, I started noticing things on my walks that were natural and pleasant smelling. In fact, walking in my neighborhood, there were some bushes or plants that I not only started to touch because of the texture, but, after touching them, I would put my fingers up to my nose to smell them, and be delighted by the smell.

Lavender, Rosemary, Basil, Eucalyptus, Roses, (Although very few roses smell anymore. In trying to figure out why, I came to learn that the scent has been genetically modified right out of them), Citrus Blossoms, Gardenias, Jasmine, Oranges, Grapefruits, Lemons... Everywhere I turned there was something to smell in my neighborhood. Opportunities to not only use but excite my sense of smell were all around me, but I had not been aware. Some I touched and smelled or picked and smelled, and some I just leaned toward to smell. Some I would even take home with me to smell again later and excite my senses all over again and also remind me of the outdoors, and my walk earlier in the day with Ciccina.

I was reminded as I started this "practice," that my Italian Father used to come home with little flowers or leaves in his hands, and sometimes they had been crushed. I wondered as a child why he had them in his hand, and as far as the crushed ones, what he had done with them and why. Later I made it a point to pay attention to what that was about. Walking around on future occasions with him, I noticed him pick something without drawing attention to the fact that he had done it, in other words, like it was second nature, not special. Depending on what it was, he would smell it right away, or crush it or break it or peel it, whatever was appropriate, to bring out the scent. As we walked he would talk and on occasion bring his hand up to his nose and smell.

In fact, my father almost always had a dried up jasmine flower or two in his car. I think he chose Jasmine for at least four reasons. One reason was because they were very fragrant. Another reason was that he liked the smell. Three, we had them in our yard. And probably the most important of them all, because it reminded him of Sicily, where he was born and raised.

Did I dismiss this at the time as weird or old fashioned? Probably. I shutter to think. Would I have preferred instead that he had a little cardboard cutout of a pine tree that had been soaked in some kind of man-made chemical hanging from the rear view mirror, or a little bottle of chemicals placed on the dashboard? At the time? Probably.

What had I done with the joy of smelling that my Father used to have and probably my ancestors did too? If I had to think about it, I bet my ancestors, and all our ancestors used their sense of smell for survival in some way. When in Italy as a young man, I remember some of the "old-timers" saying things like "It smells like rain," or "It smells like it's going to be a hot day." Could Ciccina tell the weather from her sense of smell?

It is said that dogs can smell fear. Fear? Really? And I had been wasting my sense of smell smelling fake potpourri and bathroom sprays when I could have been sniffing out fear? I wished Ciccina could teach me to smell fear. But in the meantime, she was connecting me, or I should say, reminding me, of my sense of smell again and all this from a beautiful little dog who was just going about her life, in the moment, with me.

It was time to bring back my sense of smell. Soon after these lessons, whenever I was making some food in the kitchen or whenever I was walking or..., I stopped to smell something. I don't mean, I happened to smell something, I mean, I made a point to stop and smell and see what I could smell, how it made me feel, what it made me think about, or not think about.... I found out that life can smell good and it was good to smell!

I was feeling more alive than ever. My senses were more alive, at least two of them, maybe three, and revived again. I didn't know whether touching real stuff transferred something into me or if the natural smells were doing something chemically to my brain, or if it was having Ciccina around, but I was feeling happier and more in touch, and more present than ever. Could this be part of the secret of being in the now?

12 SENSING...THERE'S MORE TO LIFE

There were definite times when Ciccina did things she was not supposed to and I felt like she was definitely not "connecting" to what was right or good for her. Like the times I would find her chewing on something I had a feeling she should not have been chewing. Sometimes I would pull Ciccina to me and hold her down while I extracted things from her mouth. I didn't think she would have swallowed every such thing but I didn't think they should have been in her mouth to begin with. I used to think and say out loud, "What are you doing?" and "What are you eating?"

The first couple times, the words "You stupid dog," came out during one of these episodes. It came, "naturally." It was something we kids used to say to each other growing up all the time. It was something that I used in reference to myself every once in a while when I felt I had done something "stupid."

It was something that I had become aware of some time previously, and I had tried to stop it, but it still slipped out every once in a while. I didn't like calling anybody stupid, and my Ciccina didn't deserve it either. I also was feeling like she could understand me and I her, and it felt like when I called her that, it made her feel bad. Besides, Ciccina was anything but stupid.

I still didn't know why she put some things in her mouth. Sometimes, she would put things in her mouth and then after a few chews, spit them out. I began to see this as tasting thing. She was tasting. Tasting. What a concept. Now one would think that I had been in touch with my sense of taste all my life, especially with my Italian Mamma who cooked amazing tasting dishes and meals. For the most part I was in touch with tasting, especially because I liked to cook and I made things that tasted really good.

Either by force of habit, or because I was so busy, or both, more often than not, even when cooking, I would be making whatever I would be making, in a hurry. When I finally got to eating, I'd wolf it down. I might even have been bypassing my taste buds. No need to taste, I already knew it tasted good, because I made it to taste the way I liked it. I gave myself license to bypass my senses, texture, taste, temperature, etc., take big bites, big swallows and be off on my way to something that I thought was "more important."

This of course references the times when I actually cooked something for myself. When I didn't have time to do that, I would buy something at a store that was already cooked, more often than not, overcooked, possibly over processed and most likely chemically laden. I wasn't even eating fast food at the time, to me, that would have been a whole other thing. Especially with fast food, I had already come to understand that most of what I used to eat, because I did eat lots of fast food and lots of processed foods for years, were scientifically engineered to taste "like" something and to artificially stimulate certain areas of our tongues and brains to make us "think" we are eating something that tastes good. Moreover, they are supposedly made to be addictive.

I was "addicted" to food as it was. I didn't need any help from chemicals and additives. But even in my "addiction," I wasn't getting the benefit of the foods I was eating, cooked foods, fast foods or processed foods, I would eat them all quickly. Eating was a task to get done as quickly as possible.

Especially when I was cooking or preparing the food myself, I could have been using my senses, the textures of the food, the smells of cooking, or spices and herbs added, the eventual taste of all the combinations, etc. It was all there for me to enjoy. It wouldn't have cost me more money, or that much more time. All that was required was a moment of awareness.

Did I enjoy the crunchy sounds of fresh pepper being ground, or salt being shaken? Did I get as much as I could from the sound of the knife blade hitting the cutting board or my vegetables being chopped? Did I take time to sense the sizzle of something in the sauté pan? And touching upon the sixth sense, what was I thinking while I am cooking? How was I feeling? Were there good thoughts coming from the process and going into the process?

These questions apply not just to the process of cooking, but also to the journey of life, moment by moment.

Finally, when it came to tasting, just like Ciccina tasting something and spitting it out, there was tasting for the sake of tasting. This was something I was well aware of, but it had never entered my consciousness as a possibility for me. I had grown up with a taster. My Mother was a taster. If she saw something edible that was interesting to her, she would taste it for the sake of tasting.

I recall she would be offered a whole piece of things while visiting friends or family, and she would say, "No, thank you, I'd like just a taste." I never understood that as a child. Why taste a piece of cake, when I could have a whole piece? Well, that was me as a child. As an adult, I still didn't taste for tasting sake, and I still didn't see it being relevant in my life. But it would have been.

This is where the food addiction thing came in. I may have been addicted to food, but I might have been more addicted to eating. I remember when I was encouraged to fast for the purpose of a body cleanse, one particular fast required I not eat any food at all for a few days. The first time I did that I walked around at about the times I would normally have been eating wanting to eat.

Of course the first couple days I was starving and so it was understandable. But after a couple of days, I was no longer as hungry but I still had the strong desire to eat for the sake of eating. And therein lies the main problem with the addiction. I was eating just to eat. I was addicted to eating.

Also, because of the types of foods that I was craving before the cleanse and fast, I was craving foods that were not the healthiest of foods. Because of all this, I thought that when I was done with the fast and cleanse, that I would eat everything in sight. But the opposite happened. To break the fast, I made myself a salad. The vegetables, greens, tomatoes, etc. never tasted so good. I was tasting and it all tasted so good and satisfying. After a small serving, I was full.

Although, unfortunately, before long I went back to my old habits. I learned and was reminded by Ciccina, the art of tasting just for tasting. There are times when I believe my body craves a sweet or salt, or alcohol, or whatever it is. There are times when a taste will satisfy me. If I take in the whole experience and take in the smell, the taste, the sensations, etc., I will find myself being satisfied with just a taste or a couple of tastes. And the whole experience having been more satisfying and pleasurable than eating a whole this or drinking a whole bottle of that.

I also learned later on, the more studying I did on these subjects, that sometimes when my body was craving something, it was not necessarily craving the particular food itself, but a nutrient that the body could absorb within the food itself. I learned that by taking certain supplements, minerals and vitamins, my cravings for sweets and savory treats was greatly curbed, for example. Though under "normal" circumstances, these nutrients would have been in the food I was eating, but alas, they supposedly weren't. And hence I was caught in a vicious cycle and luckily at least helped by dietetic education and nutrients.

In the midst of all of this period of learning, I went to a friend's wedding. At dinner a salad was served with a beautiful orchid placed on top. Where before I might have thought this was a lovely idea and a beautiful presentation, taking a page out of Ciccina's book, I asked the server if the Orchid was edible.

When I was told that it was, without batting an eyelash, I plopped the orchid in my mouth, much to everyone at the table's amazement and to some, their disgust. "Well, how does it taste?" I was asked.

It is interesting to me that many times I watched Ciccina chew on something and wondered "how does it taste?" too scared or not curious enough to actually find out for myself. I lived vicariously through the dog, at times, in a sense. And in this particular instance, my friends were living vicariously through me, too scared or not curious enough to find out for themselves, how an orchid tasted. How much of life were they missing, how much of it had I missed all those years?

I chewed away in delight while my friends at the table watched and wondered. Eating an orchid was new to all of us at the time, but more importantly than the orchid alone, this was part of a new way of living for me.

I was not in delight just from the taste of the orchid, per se, maybe orchids were an acquired taste, but I was delighted that I was chewing on it for the sake of tasting something new, something outside my comfort zone. I was using my sense of taste for something that I had never tasted before and to me. it felt like more than tasting an orchid, I was tasting LIFE.

No more did I have to wonder how life "tasted," I had a sense, a sense of taste, that I could use to taste LIFE any time I wanted to, and at that moment I decided I would taste it any chance I got!

What else was Ciccina doing? What other senses did she use?

Ciccina was always looking, looking, looking, and looking. I would say to her often, "What are you looking at, huh?" and waited as if she was going to answer verbally. She would look at me when I was speaking with her, and then she would turn away and look. Just look. Maybe she would hear something, maybe she wouldn't, maybe she was seeing something, and maybe something caught her attention or peaked her curiosity? Whatever it was, Ciccina would look.

The sense of sight I thought would be an easy sense to examine because I used my eyes all day long, and I could see things. It was quite obvious. I think I relied on my eyes and therefore my sense of sight more than any other sense. I didn't think there was anything Ciccina could teach me there. But since I was in the process of examining everything, I examined the sense of sight.

What I found was that I "saw" a lot and that I "looked" a lot, but I didn't often "look" and I didn't often truly "see." This didn't make sense to me at first but that's what came to me and by now I had learned to just go with it, at least for a while.

I "looked" at my computer all day, or I could "see" people in the audience and I "looked" for things and I "saw" stuff happening. But did I really "look" and "see" people, like Ciccina did? When Ciccina looked at me, she would often look directly into my eyes or spend what seemed like hours looking at me. I wondered not only what she was looking at, but also what she saw while she was looking. Could she see something I didn't see? If she did, would I be able to see more also, if I really looked?

I started to evaluate how many times I looked at something just for the sheer pleasure of looking. As kids we could almost stare at something for hours and be fascinated by looking. As kids we could see things that adults couldn't see. We could look at clouds and see animal figures in them that others couldn't see. Sometimes we tried to help them see, and sometimes they would.

True or not, when we saw a horsey in a cloud, it was real to us and it made us feel good to discover it on our own and to share it with others. As children we could stare at a goldfish for long periods of time and see it do things that adults didn't believe were real.

Fortunately, that was my childhood, but nowadays, children are looking and seeing things almost exclusively on TV, on the Internet, video games or other electronic devices. They are experiencing "life" in 2D instead of 3D, or better yet, 4D and beyond, and with the use of the mind, and very few of their other senses. They hold something that is plastic and manufactured and they watch something that is fabricated, and unnatural. And they take in what someone else wants them to see, someone who wants to potentially be able to sell them something, whether it be an idea, a product... a plastic life.

My childhood might have allowed for watching a cloud and imagining, or a goldfish or an ant and wondering what their world was like. But what had my day-to-day life as an adult become? I would say my life was similar to the life I described for a contemporary child, only the adult version of it. I stared at a computer all day working on plastic and looking at plastic/glass. I looked up information from other people's research and used programs and tools created by other people. I watched the news and TV on the television and went to movies, albeit not as much as most of my friends, and watched other people's stories and creations in 2D and took in other people's interpretations of life.

In this day and age, I don't think there is anything particularly "wrong" with my living this way, but when I started to examine this, I wondered when was the last time that I stared at a cloud or marveled at the wonder of the ocean or stared at and wondered what an ant was up to and how and why it went about its life?

When was the last time I hung up a painting on my wall just because it was beautiful or it reminded me of something I enjoyed looking at? When was the last time I cleaned up my room or organized it or redecorated it, not because it needed dusting, or the furniture was getting old, but because I wanted to feel something new about me or life, or see something on a daily basis that had more meaning to me?

My walks with Ciccina started to become more aesthetically beautiful. Firstly, I would take roads that had more beauty to offer and secondly because I started seeing the beauty that was there all along. I hadn't noticed my neighbor had such beautiful flowers in her yard. I never noticed the trees that grew in my area and enjoyed them for what they were. I never noticed how many stars there were out on a given night or how big the moon was. Perhaps I had seen, but not noted, or looked but not seen.

Like going to an amusement park with a child, and seeing the park through the eyes and experience of the child, perhaps, I was seeing the world for the first time through the eyes of Ciccina. Curiously, Ciccina was like my "seeing eye dog," until I got my own

---

"eyesight" back. And when I finally saw the world through my new eyes, the world was good. It was so good to see the world; I wanted to share it with everyone I knew. My favorite phrase at the time was, "Can you see that?"

Finally, last and certainly not least of the five senses, there was the sense of hearing. Being a musician and a singer, hearing was very important to me. I would listen to music any chance I got. I enjoyed playing the piano and hearing the rich full sound come out of my grand piano every time I played it. It wasn't always that I felt I needed it, but every once in awhile I would remove everything off of the lid of my piano and I would lift the lid and prop it up to fill the room with the biggest sound like only a grand piano can do. At the piano, sitting at the heart of all that sound and surrounded by the music I would play, I could and often would be occupied and blissful for hours.

The world did not stop producing sounds once I stopped making sound, whether at the piano or on the stereo. Of course I could hear the TV or listen to people talk, etc. I would hear the occasional fire truck go by, buses, car alarms, and all of that. Luckily I could tune those "fabricated" sounds out after awhile. Along with tuning those out, I think I must have tuned everything else out too, either that, or I didn't know how to hear some of the sounds that I wanted to or needed to hear… for "living."

Not Ciccina. Were her senses keener than mine or was she just more connected to them? Technically, yes, and yes. Some of her senses were definitely keener than mine, or all humans for that matter. We might not want the kind of extra human sensory that is natural to dogs, anyway. But she was also keyed in to certain sounds that I could hear but I wasn't listening to, and that is what I learned I was missing and I needed.

Her ears would physically perk up for seemingly no reason at all. Thankfully mine didn't do that, because first of all, it would look weird, and secondly, I would have never gotten any work done. But when we were out for a walk, as I started to take the more scenic routes for my sense of sight, they ended up also being routes with less traffic, and I would make a point to listen when Ciccina

72

would stop to listen.

"What could she be hearing?" I would think to myself. Is it a bird? Is it a plane? If I really tuned in to her and what might be attracting her attention I would hear what I thought she was listening to. Maybe not as clearly or as loudly as she could hear it, but I could hear it. It might have been a bird, another dog, a cat, or a cricket, or a bee even.

Ah, the sounds of nature. A bird. A cricket. Once I tuned in, to these sounds of nature, a sense of calm would come over me. I would smile, or I would feel more relaxed. As a society we have what has been termed "noise pollution." After awhile, unless we pay attention to it, some of us don't even know it's there. In some areas, the noise could literally be deafening, over time, as reported about such places as the New York Subway.

Manmade noise is in fact so ubiquitous, that it is literally hard to find a place on earth that is completely without human sound of some kind over an extended period of time. Between timber operations, mining, agriculture, road, nautical shipping routes, commercial and noncommercial flights, cruise ships, military operations, etc. human "manufactured" noise is everywhere. And the areas where uninterrupted natural sounds can be heard are getting smaller and smaller, fewer and fewer.

Even where there exists human noise, we add our own, because we can't seem to live without excess noise anymore. We hear canned music in almost every office and store we go into. We keep our radios on in the car even when we are talking to people on the phone or next to us. We even keep our TVs on all morning and all night, just to have some noise, or "company," as many say.

Are these sounds really satisfying our senses? Are they really feeding our psyches, our souls, and us? Are they distractions or worse? It is as if we are afraid to be without sound.

For the most part, Ciccina didn't seem to like "manufactured" sound. I know all dogs aren't like this, but on the rare occasion that I turned on the TV, she would walk out of the room.

Depending on what music I played, she would do the same, but if it was me sitting at the piano, she would either want to be on my lap or right underneath my piano bench, at my feet, or underneath the middle of the piano's sounding board.

Was it the fact that the piano is an all-natural instrument made of wood and metal? Could it be because a human was playing it? Could it be because I was playing it? Did she like my piano music selection? I could presume to have answers to these questions, but I do know this, that like Ciccina, I was hearing and listening to the sounds of the world and tuning in more and more to its natural beauty and wanting to and needing to turn off as much of the "manufactured" noise as possible.

Like we crave foods and drinks, I found myself craving sounds. I was starting to miss hearing a bird, a cricket, a cat's purr, a dog's bark, the wind rustling the trees… Isn't there a bible verse in which Jesus says something about, man not being able to live on bread alone? Well, I was beginning to think that actual food was only a small part of what we humans needed to subsist and that most of us have been starving for so long.

I recall an Auntie Mame quote, too, about life being a banquet and most people are starving. This is how I had started feeling, like I was missing out on a world I never knew existed. But my world had opened up. Ciccina had helped me get in touch with my five senses, without which, I was beginning to realize; there is no true living and no true being.

13 A DOG'S SIXTH SENSE

Working on awakening the five senses that I already knew I had, was tough enough., Imagine trying to awaken the sixth sense, a sense I didn't know I had, much less know how to use or what to do with it.

The more and more I connected with my five senses; the more and more I was starting to feel myself, the me I felt I was meant to be. A few of the changes in me seemed to have nothing to do with my senses specifically. For example, I was more temperate, I didn't get upset as easily, I seemed to take my time more with various tasks, especially the ones that seemed menial, but allowed me an opportunity to enjoy my senses.

Was it just because I had a dog, or was it because of what I had learned from the dog? Does everyone who has a dog learn these lessons?

In the Tao, Lao Tzu is credited for saying, "When the student is ready, the teacher appears." I was never sure exactly what this meant, but I always related to this saying, for some reason. Did Lao Tzu mean, when we are ready, puff, there will be a teacher in front of us like a Genie? Did he mean that we would come across a person who would teach us things when we are ready to learn them? Could he also have meant that when we were ready, the teacher, who may have already been in front of us all along, appears to us as a teacher? In other words, we recognize him/her as the teacher.

Whichever Lao Tzu meant, I was beginning to believe that my "teacher" had appeared in the form of a dog. Could it really be that I had my own private "Yoda" like in Star Wars? Did this kind of thing really happen?

Whether Ciccina was really teaching me things, or I was just learning from paying attention to things I had never paid attention to, I was truly learning and changing for the better. I was ready for these teachings and changes. If what Lao Tzu said was true, it wasn't until I was ready to learn, that I recognized the lessons I was being taught, in this case, just by example, in a gentle, beautiful way. In fact, up until this moment, I had learned all my lessons, as my friends would say, the hard way. In my learning, I was also learning that "learning," didn't have to be hard, or come the hard way.

It is true that I knew some of what I was learning already and maybe I was just being reminded to do it again, or do more of it. And as for learning from joy, I must have tuned into that right away. I could have been miserable about this whole experience. Instead, I took it in stride. Better yet, at the moment I was relishing it for all it was worth.

It was interesting that months before I was lamenting the fact that I didn't have very many out of town performance engagements. Not only was it part of my work, but also I enjoyed being busy, traveling and singing, as I had been doing all year up to that point. But these months were like a dry spell. Is it a coincidence that if I had had out of town engagements, I would have probably not been able to keep Ciccina all this time? I would have told my family that I couldn't keep her long enough to meet everyone. I would have had to find her another home sooner, or would have had to have left her at another shelter, which I could not have imagined doing.

Had I been traveling, I would have not had the time to take as good care of Ciccina as I had. I definitely would not have had the opportunity to walk with her and take our time with each of the experiences we had. I also would not have been around to have local meetings and take her with me. Without trying to romanticize it, it truly felt like this period of my life had been divinely orchestrated.

As divinely orchestrated as it was, I was having a hard time being in the moment and allowing the flow be as it was supposed to. My thoughts vacillated between, "This is so perfect," to "When I do have to leave town, what am I going to do?" In a way, I was not getting it. If the plan had been divinely orchestrated, why would the divine abandon me in a month?

In the later part of July, I had an engagement in Milwaukee that would keep me out of town for a week. I was certain that by then, I will have had time to visit my family. Undoubtedly they would fall in love with Ciccina as I had, and they would want to adopt her. I technically had nothing to worry about. Maybe it wasn't the anxiety of finding her a home that was concerning me. Maybe, I had so come to love Ciccina that I could not bear to think about having to be without her.

I was definitely feeling like we had so many things we still had to do together. There was so much I wanted to learn and I felt like she was the one to teach me. Talk about teaching an old dog a new trick. In this case, I was the old dog, and the new dog was teaching me more than a new trick or two.

And speaking of old dogs, Ciccina wasn't old at all. Along the way, at a party, one of the guests said she was a veterinarian and took a look at her. She told me Ciccina was at the most three years old. If you ask me she was pretty wise for being only three years old.

One of the things I really wanted to learn, or get in touch with, or be reminded of, or whatever, was this sixth sense kind of stuff she used to do. For example, I used to walk toward my car where she would be waiting for me. I could not see her, which meant she was sitting somewhere on the seat or the floor. As I would start to approach she would pop her head up and her tail was already wagging as if she knew I was coming.

This happened quite often. Not every time, because I imagine sometimes she would be napping. But often enough for it to not be a fluke, she would do this. How did she know? There were times that I was wearing quiet shoes or walking on grass. Though her hearing was super dog hearing, it felt like there was something else going on. From afar, I also saw her do that with other people, however, in those cases, her tail would not be wagging, and she would be barking at them. I was convinced she knew when it was me approaching.

There were times when I would swear that she could read my mind. She would go to the door as I was thinking of taking her for a walk. It would not be at our normal walk time, but at a time when I felt I needed and could take a break.

For example, there would be times when I felt like getting something to eat and she would beat me to the refrigerator. I can't explain it really, because I can't say that I was in touch with it. Or maybe I was. Maybe I used to sense when she wanted to eat or maybe she used to send me a message somehow when she wanted to take a walk and I thought that it was coming from me.

I wasn't sure how this all worked but I wanted to find out as much as I could. I figured, Ciccina had it figured out by instinct or by whatever. I would take the opportunity to tune into whatever this was that I referred to as the sixth sense.

So what was it? How did I tap into it? How could I use it? What could I use it for? With all my questions, I couldn't help but wonder why we as people don't talk about this more, and ask these kinds of questions? I had many friends with dogs, and on occasion I would hear the kind of comment that sounded like, "I can swear he reads my mind," and other such telling comments. But as telling as those kinds of comments are, this is where the conversation would stop and we would move on to something else.

I got to wondering, if it was that obvious to me after only having a dog for a couple months, then dog owners and keepers all over the world certainly must know of this? Why don't people tap into it more? Do they think it is just for dogs? Then it dawned on me, people DO talk about this type of phenomenon all the time, they just might not talk about it like I'm thinking about it now. I have often heard stories and have seen stories on TV about dogs that traveled thousands of miles back home after being inadvertently left. I have learned of animals that have helped rescue people by sensing that there was something wrong and have alerted others.

Many animals feel earthquakes before we do. Birds fly in exact formations and herds run together and move together and turn together without bumping into each other. I could go on and on. Does this not make us think? Did it ever make me think before? Animals are connected to something that guides them beautifully through life and through their journey.

Granted sometimes on that journey a gazelle gets eaten by a lion, but that is part of life, at least at the moment, life as we know it. Or do we really know it? Who knows anymore?

What do we know if we are getting lost on our way home from the grocery store when animals can travel thousands of miles and find their way home? What do we know if we are bumping into each other in hallways and in walkways and can't move through life as easily or elegantly as herds do?

At this point, I felt that I wanted to do some learning from my new friend Dorothy, who could help answer my questions, instead of me having to figure them out with Ciccina. Ironically, she did not want to answer my questions. She instead told me I had to experience it and that she was so excited that I had finally asked her.

She told me, she knew this time would come and that what I needed was to "fly with her on the table." "Flying on the Table," was the way she described one of her healing modalities. According to her, this modality, amongst others, helped people connect with their Higher selves. Once connected we are in tune with all the answers and the answers we need to live our best life. I looked forward to a "ride on the table," but Dorothy lived in San Diego and I in Los Angeles, and I needed answers right away. I began to call Dorothy more frequently and tried to slip the questions I had in between the conversation. Dorothy knew what

I was doing. My thinking mind was getting the better of me. Some things needed to be experienced and not explained. She weeded out the "monkey mind" questions, and answered the ones that she wanted to, temporarily appeasing my mind, yet not spoiling the greater learnings I would experience or come to know.

"Ciccina is going too fast," I heard myself say during one such call, as if Ciccina was speeding through the course agenda. Was it coming at me too fast or was I opening up to it more and more? What more could there be? How long would this go on?

There was so much to talk about, in my mind at least, and before long Dorothy and my Ciccina talks on the phone became almost a nightly occurrence. I was sensing that I was truly connecting with something that was at the same time, familiar and yet completely new to me. I was no longer sure if this was a sixth sense thing, or if it was something else. All I knew was that things that were out of the norm were starting to happen, and/or I was becoming more aware of them, the things that were out of the "norm." They weren't necessarily big things, they were small, at least at first, but they were not "normal," or real, and they were thought provoking.

It got to the point that I could no longer keep these things to myself or share them just with Dorothy. I began sharing it with my family and many of my friends. It got to the point where every one of my conversations, outside of business, and even then, had the undertone of "the meaning of life," my changing life.

14 THE MEANING OF... A DOG'S LIFE

The more I contemplated the meaning of life, the more my life changed. The more my life changed, the more I contemplated the meaning of life. And with the contemplating came questions, lots of questions. What didn't seem to come as readily were the answers to my questions. Or did they? Once again it was quite possible that the answers were directly in front of me all the time.

I wasn't sure about that, but I was looking at it this way, I, the student, was ready, and my teacher, at least for the time being, had appeared, so I turned to her, Ciccina, once again for the answers.

Sometimes I wished I could talk to her. If she could talk back, she could just tell me the answers to my questions. Of course, if she could talk, then she might have questions of her own. The experience would be completely different and at the moment I was thinking that it would be a better one. Yet, if dogs could talk, would we want them around? If dogs could communicate with us like we humans do, then maybe we wouldn't have the same kind of experience as we currently do with dogs and cats and other domesticated animals.

Maybe the special relationship we have with domesticated animals is special because they don't talk. But talking and communicating are two completely different things. We communicate really well with our pets; at least I believe most of us do. In many cases, maybe we communicate even better with our pets than we do with our fellow humans. I wonder if maybe the problems that some of us have with human communication is, ironically, that we talk, or maybe it's that we talk too much? What a concept?

Would the world be a better place and human relationships be more harmonious if we communicated more silently with each other, instead of relying so much on talking? As strange as this sounded, it actually made sense to me. But what wasn't clear was exactly what that "silent" communication was. Was it the sixth sense? Was this where that kind of communication happened?

For lack of a better term, I will refer to the "place" where we communicate silently as the sixth sense. At the time, the sixth sense was a loose concept to me. I recognized that there was much more to communication than what we say to each other, though most people, I have found, consider this the most important part. I had already learned that "body language" could sometimes be more important than what the person was actually saying.

In a similar way, I was learning that listening is sometimes a more important part of communication than talking.

Therefore, the part of communication that was visible, as in body language, and audible as in listening, I knew was definitely a part of communicating. But was it a part of the sixth sense? There was so much more than what met the eyes and ears to this communication thing. A funny thought came to mind. Is the act of talking sometimes getting in the way of a better way of communicating? Even when one is actively listening in a conversation, it inherently means that someone has to be talking.

So what could be better than talking or listening when it came to communicating? Could it be feeling? Could it be connecting? If it were connecting; connecting to what? To whom? Where does this connecting take place? Is that place the place that some scientists have referred to as the ether?

This reminded me of something that happened in Jr. High School, just before I went to High School. As part of trying to get the "rival" magnet Junior High Schools to "integrate" before the students of each school came together in High School, a handful of student leaders or influencers were chosen from each Jr. High School and taken through a ropes course together.

At the time I didn't see myself as either a leader or an influencer, but obviously someone did, and so I got to go. The course was one of the highlights of my entire school experience. I wish the whole class could have been able to take it, or better yet, the whole school, students, teachers, and administrators. In fact, I think it could have been an actual course taught at the High School. Knowing what I know now, it would have made such a big difference in the lives of all the students. I know it did on mine.

Maybe it influenced my life because I used it as an analogy for so many different areas of my life. I liked every part of the course. I wasn't good at every part of the course, but I liked it all. One part in particular made the most impact on me and was the most memorable. I am referring to the exercise in which we all had to scale a wall. The wall was too high for anyone of us to even touch the top, so we needed a boost.

Obviously this was a team building exercise and we were timed as we did it. I don't remember how long it took us, but I do remember that there was a lot of arguing in the process and comments like "No, not like that, this way," and "I can't do that." Granted, not all of us were in shape to be able to easily, physically do this, even with help from our fellow teammates. Some of us were heavy, or not physically capable, so it wasn't easy getting the whole team over the wall.

The thing that I remember most about the experience was that we had to do it twice. We did not know this the first time we did it. After all the cheering and congratulations, the course facilitators told us that we were going to have to do it all over again. Not because we had done it wrong, but because we were going to do it differently the second time.

We couldn't believe it, especially since some of us were tired, and couldn't understand what the purpose was, since we had just done it. There was a catch. The catch was that the second time we had to do it completely silent, without talking. If anyone spoke even one word, we would all have to start all over again.

You can imagine our disbelief in our ability to be able to complete this task.

Did we do it? Not only did we do it, we did it without speaking even one word and having to start over again. And not only that, we were able to do it in much less time than the first time we did it. We did it without complaining and without discussing and without being able to plan. Once they told us the rules, we were told to stop the talking and get started and from then on we got creative with non-verbal communication.

Sure we had just done it, so we knew "physically" we could do it, and pretty much how to do it, but it's not as if we did it the exact same way the second time. Some of the same people did some of the same things, and took some of the same positions but it wasn't all the same. We were a very large group, so it wasn't as if we even remembered exactly who went over before or after whom.

Afterwards, I personally was amazed that it could be done without talking and amazed at the kind of non-verbal communication we made-up on the fly, and the way we effectively used it. When it was all said and done, I was convinced that had we been able to talk the second time, it would have taken us longer and we wouldn't have done it as well. I wonder what it would have been like if we had been asked to scale the wall non-verbally the first time?

You should have been there to hear the exhilaration we all felt at the end of the no talking exercise. It did not compare to the previous feeling. Maybe it was because we had never done anything like that before, or maybe because we were so surprised that we actually could do it? Or maybe it was also because we had not been able to talk throughout the whole exercise that we had a lot of things to say afterwards? Or maybe in that non-verbal communication, we were needing to use a different sense or "communicating" in a different way? Maybe we were "connecting" in a way more powerful than any way we had known, with each other?

I wondered what could be the reason I was being reminded of this and what this might have to do with Ciccina and everything I was learning? Surely we have a mouth and have developed language capabilities for a reason, but are we using our mouths and language capabilities effectively?

An analogy came to mind that helped put this into perspective. Before the many recording devices we currently had, one of the first video recording device was BETA technology. BETA video recording devices were introduced into part of the world market a year or so before VHS, a competing video recording device, was introduced, as I understand it. According to many, BETA recording devices were better than VHS, but only a few years afterwards, VHS was still going strong and BETA's were starting to be phased out. According to some, it was because of a good marketing strategy from the company that made VHS, or more dollars spent on advertising, or something like that.

Therefore, to extend the analogy, speaking with our mouths might be like VHS. It gets a lot of publicity, especially these days in school, and from our parents, eager for us to learn words. It is what is taught in schools and used in many organizations and corporations. But what if speaking with our mouths isn't the best mode of communication and was never intended to be our primary mode of communication? What if speaking, like VHS, is inferior to BETA, like our Sixth Sense, and BETA/Sixth Sense is discounted because VHS/talking gets more attention.

It is a crazy, unconventional thought, to be sure, but nonetheless, have we ever stopped to think about that? I sure hadn't. This reminds me of seeing old people sitting on their front porches in small towns or in pictures or movies, and noticing that they rarely are saying very much to each other. They just sat there.

Sometimes you see old couples just holding hands or looking at each other. Sometimes you see old people just sitting side by side, on park benches or in coffee shops, etc. Are they doing that because they have nothing to say to each other? Perhaps. Are they doing it because they are too old and tired to talk? Perhaps. Are they doing that because they have said so much in life they already know what each other is going to say? Perhaps. Or do they know something we don't know? And do they even know that they know what they might know?

Is there another form of communication, and could it be better than using our talking abilities? Growing up, we had our Grandmother, Sara, living with us since before I was born. Incidentally, it was her sister in Italy, our Great Aunt, who also had the name Ciccina. Our Grandmother, Sara, lived to be 99 years and 11 months young. She was young until the last few years of her life; until she fell and was bedridden in our home almost until the end.

When my Grandmother fell her final time and became bedridden, my Mother became her 24-hour caretaker. She was taking 24-hour care of the house, my father, (who was starting to fall ill at that time), our Grandmother, and still finding time to spend time with us, her children, making sure everyone was doing well. This went on for years until my Mother also fell and injured her knee. She became bedridden herself for a short time. During that time, my Grandmother had to be taken to a nursing home, something my Mother never wanted to have happen, and fought against it, until it became inevitable because of her inability to care for her.

Almost immediately, upon my Grandmother being placed in the nursing home, her physical body started to deteriorate quickly.

When we realized this, all of the Grandchildren traveled to visit her. On one such visit, my Uncle, my Grandmother's son, Gaspare, traveled to see her as well. During his stay in town, he went to see her several times. During one of those times, he and my Father decided to go together and they asked me if I wanted to go along with them. I went with them. Unbeknownst to me, it would be the last time I that would see my Grandmother.

When we got to the nursing home we were all shocked to see how far gone she was and how far removed she felt from this world. We approached her and I remember my Uncle, her son, trying to get her attention. She had her eyes closed and didn't respond to him, didn't open her eyes and made no sign of recognizing him. My Father, her son-in-law, whom she loved as her own, tried to get her attention as well and was saddened by the fact that she was not recognizing him either.

Myself, I just stood there with my eyes tearing up. I figured if she didn't recognize her own son and son-in-law, she probably wouldn't recognize or acknowledge me either. I just watched with sadness as they tried speaking to her and tried to get her to look at them. My Grandmother's only response was to babble, while her head and eyes wandered and never fixed on any point, least of all, on them.

All of a sudden I remembered that I had read something crazy about the soul. I remember reading that the soul resides three feet above the body, or something like that. To this day, I don't know if that is true or not and don't even recall where I learned it. For some reason, this came to mind and it rang true at that moment.

Based on that, I figured, if "talking" to her "body" wasn't working for two of her favorite people in the world, I would try "talking" to her soul. I remembered too that animals supposedly communicate with mental pictures and that good animal communicators and trainers use mental images to get messages across to them. Armed with those two pieces of information, I stood to the side of my Grandmother's bed, held her hand and directed my gaze three feet above her head.

I then proceeded to visualize many wonderful times she and I had had together in my young life. I then verbally, but in my head, thanked her for all she had shared with me and taught me. I thanked her for being the best Grandmother she could have possibly been to me and told her that if it was her time to go and she felt she had to go, then I would understand and would support her in that. I ended my communication with my Nonna, as we called her, with "I will miss you and will always remember you for the rest of my life. Ti voglio bene Nonna (I love you Nonna)."

As soon as I was done, I looked down at my Grandmother's face and through my blurred vision due to my eyes filled with tears, I saw my Grandmother's eyes fix and then lock on to mine and stare into them for what seemed like an eternity. Simultaneously, while she loving held my gaze, the biggest smile came over her face, and serenity came over her and us.

I could tell that my Father and Uncle were amazed and I heard them comment, though I didn't pay attention to what they said, I was somewhere else. I couldn't believe what had just happened. I wasn't sure if I was happier that I had made a connection with my Grandmother or that I had tried something crazy that just popped into my head, at the perfect time, and it actually worked.

I never told either my Father or my Uncle what I had done; I thought they would think I was crazy. But my Grandmother proved to me that I wasn't. Most importantly, in that moment, I couldn't have been more grateful for my having been able to say goodbye in a most special way. I had also come away with a life lesson I would never forget and use in more ways than I could have imagined at that time.

This lesson was also a reminder that things like this have happened to me all my life. But it wasn't until Ciccina came around that I was reminded of this. It was something that I always took in stride. It was something that I didn't allow as part of my life. It could have had a lot to do with the fact that when I would mention these kinds of things I would be laughed at, or worse, scolded. These were things that the adults around me either did not understand or probably scared them. Because of this, I allowed them to scare me too, and try to forget.

Perhaps therein lay the answer to my question about the billions of pet owners. I wondered if others experienced similar things like I had, and had learned similar things from those experiences because of having and caring for a pet. Maybe like me, many pet owners had experienced and learned many things from their pets, but maybe these were things people just didn't talk about or maybe even understand and maybe they were forgotten, or chalked up to coincidence, or funny things that happen with pets.

I had been taking all these experiences in stride, until that time. I decided it was time to "get it." I figured I had asked for it, and I was convinced more than ever that Ciccina was one of the answers to my many prayers, and/or at least, my "teacher" in that moment, to help me get to the answers.

Each time I felt like I had received a big "gift" from Ciccina, I felt like I needed to thank her, or reward her with "something." I would either buy her a toy or a cool treat or a prettier collar or something. After all, she had given me so much already; I had to do something for her. Of course, most of these things didn't mean much to her. She just wanted to be with me. She didn't care what kind of collar she was wearing or if she had another toy. I started to see how I was imposing on our relationship between man and dog, what many people do in their relationships; that is, give each other gifts of things they really don't need and sometimes don't want, over what they really need, togetherness, time, love.

I remember finding it odd the first time it happened that I would be playing with Ciccina and I would stop to give her a treat. She didn't take the treat and instead wanted to keep on playing. Even if it had been one of her favorite treats. The treat she was enjoying, playing with me, was a bigger treat to her. It made me pause and take note. She would eat the treat when we were done playing.

As happens with many things, jobs, relationships, etc., Ciccina and I got into a routine. I needed to get back to working more and fussing over her a little less. Before long, I had gotten into my work routine again, and though I paid attention to Ciccina, it wasn't like the first couple days wherein we had spent all day together. Actually, we still spent all day together but I wasn't playing with her, fussing over her, or marveling at her like I did at the beginning.

Whenever we would play, she would just eat that all up. I enjoyed it too. And if I got up and took the time to get her a treat, I guess she figured that I might have the time to play too, so she would leave the treat and jump all over me. She would even leave the toys, as she wasn't much for toys. All she wanted was me, a REAL being, a personal connection.

Was there a lesson here for me? Maybe I had been doing it all wrong. So much of my life revolved around things. Even my focusing on my career was my focusing on things, awards, Cds, houses, cars. I was working so I could have things. I loved singing and music very much. I loved entertaining. I loved the audiences and the fans. I loved radio hosting. I worked hard to get better at my craft in each aspect of my career, but somehow those were not the rewards, in my mind, the rewards were the things I could buy after the experiences. Or, at least, I was using the things as a measure as to how well I had done up to that point.

At the same time, almost everything I was doing was starting to not be fun anymore because I was feeling like I hadn't achieved enough of the things that I thought I had to achieve and still hadn't. I was down on myself because, in my mind, I hadn't achieved enough things, recognition, made enough money, etc. Even though my desire to have more money only meant that I could spend more on the people I loved, something was not right. The people I loved wanted a relationship with me more than they wanted me to spend money on them. That's the kind of beautiful people that I had and have in my life, but I wasn't getting it.

As I analyzed this further, I realized I wanted money and things so I could spend it on, and gift the people in my life. Even if I was going to enjoy some of this money or things with them, my focus was not on the people in my life. Ciccina did not need things to enjoy me. In fact, I would wake up grumpy on some mornings, get out of bed in my old pajamas, with my hair a mess. She loved me anyway. Ciccina, didn't care how I looked, what I wore, what I bought her, how much money I made, how many houses I owned, how many awards I had received. Ciccina didn't care about anything but ME, and loved me unconditionally just the way I was.

There I was saying I want to do things with people I loved but I wasn't even loving the people I loved the way Ciccina loved me. For example, on the occasion when I would be going out with my Mother, I wanted her to dress up "nice." I would "politely" say, "are you going out in that?" I would guilt her into wearing something she wasn't comfortable in and didn't want to wear, just so that I could take her out so SHE could have a good time. I was more concerned with "what people would say," or what I thought was the proper way to dress to go to the places I was taking her, than how my Mother felt about it.

Never once did Ciccina say to me, "You are not touching me until you shower," or "You're taking me for a walk dressed like that?" I never noticed Ciccina's face change when I came out of the shower naked without the benefit of clothes hiding my excess weight that I myself couldn't stand looking at in the mirror. She wagged her tail and smiled, in her beautiful way, jumped with excitement, and never once treated me any differently. She always treated me lovingly. In a way, maybe she loved me more than I loved myself?

When I was grumpy, however, she left me alone, or she tried to cheer me up. And it worked, for the most part. When I was happy, she was right there with me. When I was down, she picked me up. When I needed her, without knowing I needed her, she never abandoned me for her toys. In fact, eventually, I stopped "rewarding" her with toys and treats. I figured it out. Those weren't for her, those were for me, to trick me into thinking I was doing something good for her. But all she wanted was food, water, walks and me. How simple and how beautiful was that? How easy?

Ciccina wanted nothing plastic, nothing fake, and nothing meaningless. She didn't understand that she was driving in the lap of luxury in my Mercedes Benz, she was just as happy when we got into some of my friends' cars, cars that didn't have a fancy hood ornament. She didn't jump all over women when we were in Beverly Hills who had designer bags or labels on their jeans, she just jumped for joy when she saw people who were genuine and who loved animals and could notice her and give each other love.

What was wrong with her? Better yet, what was wrong with me? What had I bought into all these years, and what was I supposed to do with the new found knowledge?

15 TAKING MY GIRL TO MEET MY MOTHER

The time had finally come for Ciccina to meet the family. I was a bit nervous. "What if they don't like her?" I thought to myself. It was as if I was "bringing a girl home to meet my Mother," and in a way, I was. Ciccina was very much a girl, but a girl dog. Another difference was I wasn't hoping that Mom would approve of my girl, I was hoping my Mom would adopt her. If my Mom didn't want to adopt her, then I was hoping one of my brothers or maybe my sister would.

I gave Ciccina a good spa day with all the trimmings, literally; again, this was more for me than for her, although I thought she liked being clean. Regardless, she was all clean and fresh and pretty. I packed myself three bags for the couple of days stay, and a small bag of food and bowls for the little one, and off we went on our first extended road trip together. While driving I got to thinking, maybe I packed more than most people would have packed for such a short trip? When I compared what I brought for Ciccina and what I brought for myself, all of a sudden my three bags seemed a bit excessive.

My life was different than a dog's life, granted, but did my life have to be that much more cluttered and cumbersome? How far removed from the simplicity of life had I gotten? These questions made me realize that there were more changes I would be making in the near future in yet another area of my life, the travel department. Destination... "traveling lighter!"

Ciccina was great on the trip, such great company too. I had made that trek to my Mother's house for years back and forth by myself. It was good to have company. In fact, it had become good to have company period. I had gotten quite used to it. But knowing my traveling schedule would be picking up, and for many other reasons, maybe more in my head kind of reasons than real life reasons, I knew I wouldn't be able to have Ciccina's company for long.

When Ciccina and I arrived at my Mother's door, she was greeted with lots of love and attention. Cheers and greetings and pettings and loving, she took it all in. I felt like we had both hit the jackpot. I had done my "job" and kept her a month longer for the family, and Ciccina had found her new home.

The days we spent together at my Mother's were a dream. The whole family joyously took turns taking care of Ciccina. My little nieces especially were glued to her. They and the dog were inseparable the whole time we were together. This was it, home at last. "We did it Ciccina," I thought, things couldn't be better and more perfect. I had learned everything I needed to learn and now my family had a new dog and Ciccina had a happy, loving family and home. I would also get to see Ciccina and spend time with her every time I visited my Mother, or one of my siblings, whomever ended up adopting her.

We all had so much fun together, I had never seen Ciccina play so much and eat so much. She got to experience her "Italian roots" with all the delicious Italian meals my Mother made. For Ciccina every meal was abbondanza, and bowl lickin' good.

I remember calling my friends, Dorothy and Laura, while I was away and telling them the good news. Laura was happy for me and for Ciccina, though she still couldn't get her name right after all this time, and she hoped Ciccina's new family would change it soon. We laughed about it and I told her that there was no chance of that, Ciccina had taken to the name and my nieces really liked it.

Laura had been concerned about finding Ciccina a new home, and a new name, too. She had insisted on helping me find her a home because she knew the dog was special and wanted a special home for her. I had told her that my family was going to be taking her and that made us both happy.

On the other hand, I found it interesting to hear Dorothy on the phone be surprised when I told her that my brother and sister-in-law decided they wanted Ciccina. They had seen how good Ciccina was with their daughters, and how much their daughters loved her. Dorothy really didn't know any of them well and had no reason to doubt them or what I was saying. And yet Dorothy responded to my news by telling me that she didn't think this was the end of the road for Ciccina and I, and that she wouldn't be surprised if I came back home with the dog.

I didn't think Dorothy understood how important it was that I found Ciccina a home right away. It was by now the end of June and in a few weeks I would need to fly to Milwaukee to sing at a festival for a week. This festival also signaled the start of the festival season for me. I would be singing at several festivals around the country and be doing a lot of traveling and would not be able to take Ciccina with me.

I told Dorothy that I was happy my brother and sister-in-law wanted Ciccina, and that I wasn't planning on coming back home with her. Dorothy mumbled something like "I know what I know," and we said our goodbyes and I hung up the phone, a bit puzzled by our conversation. Shortly thereafter, my brother and sister-in-law sat me down to talk. They told me that they were happy and pleasantly surprised that the dog was everything I described her to be. She really took to the children and the children to her and they all got along famously. They told me that they would happily adopt Ciccina and find a way to make it work.

I felt really good about this and couldn't wait to tell Dorothy, it was done. Instead, as it turned out, during our visit together, my brother and sister-in-law subsequently received a large work contract that included several engagements, which would mean more travel than they had even planned for the upcoming year. This shook them out of their reverie and brought them back to reality. It would have been hard taking Ciccina as it was, and they were going to make it work, but with this new contract it just wouldn't be possible and it wouldn't be right for Ciccina either. They wouldn't be able to travel with her to the hotels and they wouldn't want to leave her behind.

Maybe Dorothy was right after all, maybe this wasn't the end of the road for Ciccina and I? Afterwards I had a conversation with my Mother and it was obvious that she couldn't have a dog in her life, even if it was perfect Ciccina. It was also not the right time for my sister to have a dog in hers. I did end up traveling back home with the dog, just as Dorothy had told me.

On the seat next to me or on my lap, on the drive home, as happy as I was to have Ciccina with me, my anxiety was starting to escalate to find her a home. In my mind, the search was officially on again for a home for Ciccina. I wasted no time, while on the road, I made phone calls. The first person I called was Laura. I told her what had happened and she assured me that with her connections in the community of animal lovers, she knew she would find Ciccina the perfect home.

I wasn't pawning this off on Laura, as I saw it, I really trusted her when it came to things like this. She was able to connect and really feel people and situations and know when things would work out right and who would be right. She had rescued dogs and had many friends who had done the same. I knew that it wasn't the easiest task for her at that moment because of having recently lost two dogs of her own, but she volunteered and I was so grateful she had. I knew she was doing it not only because of her love for me, but also for her strong love for Ciccina.

There was so much I needed to do before I was ready for Festival Season and having Laura offer to find Ciccina a home was one thing less I had to worry about. I had long given up on the couple I met that day Ciccina and I first met. I had not heard back from them after our first couple of conversations. I figured that they thought they had done the most they could do. Or maybe they knew, too, that Ciccina and I had a story we had to live out, and we were living it.

And speaking of "living," if there was one thing I felt like I was doing more at that point than in most of my life, it was just that, LIVING. My new found way to live was something I never wanted to let go of. Ciccina in my future or no Ciccina in my future, this was what life was going to be about for me from that point on.

16 HAPPY FOURTH OF JULY

It's interesting how we say we believe things, and then when we are tested on our beliefs, sometimes almost immediately afterwards, we fail the test, sometimes completely negating what we had just said. What I am referring to specifically, in this case, is the "living" thing. I was one who often went to parties and events and had a very active social life, but it was a "business" sort of social life. I went to parties and events knowing I was going to get this or that out of it, or knowing I had to go because this person would be there or that it would be good for business. I rarely, if ever did things for the purpose of "living," or having a good time. I just didn't have time for that, or so I thought. I had gotten into the bad habit of trying to figure out why I needed to go somewhere or do something and not just doing something just to do it, for the sake of doing, for the sake of being, for the sake of... living.

Just as quickly as I had decided that I was going to be "living" for the sake of living, I passed up on every opportunity to do just that. I was busily getting ready to go sing a new show in Milwaukee in about a week and a half. Besides everything I needed to do, I had still not found Ciccina a home. I had every intention of working, as was my modus operandi up to the hour of my flight, pulling all-nighters if I had to, to get things perfect or as right as I could make them.

In the midst of all this came the Fourth of July and a day off and a day of celebration and parties for most of my friends and family, but as far as I was concerned, not for me. I felt like I needed to work. Working on a Holiday was actually a good work day, as I saw it, in the sense that if everyone else had the day off, that meant I wouldn't be getting business phone calls, and could get lots of work done.

Up came the test. I got invited to six Fourth of July parties, between family and friends. Not one, not two, but six. From barbeques, to pool parties to fireworks watching parties. Soon after I had promised myself I was going to live just to live, I turned down every single one of the invitations and opportunities to "live just to live." I was grateful to have so many people love me and think of me and want to have me at their parties, but I felt that it was more important to get "work" done at home rather than just having fun with my family and friends. That's how I saw it at the time.

The idea of living just for living, that which I had made a point of wanting to incorporate in my life, went out the window. Had not Ciccina taught me anything? Had I not learned? Apparently I had not learned, or at least not this particular lesson. I did take some time however to wish some of my family, friends and associates a Happy Fourth on the phone.

Most of my friends knew that I was not big on celebrating Holidays, or it being compulsory that they be celebrated on a designated day. Maybe this had to do with the fact that sometimes Holidays come around at the most "inopportune" time, according to my way of thinking at the time? Maybe it's because I had seen too many people do silly things just to celebrate something on a particular day, when in my opinion, celebrating the next day, would have been just as good if not better?

Birthdays, for instance, are great because people tend to think of their friends and loved ones on their Birthdays. But there are people who get offended if someone doesn't think of them on their Birthday. I'm not one of these people. The way I look at it, if any day of the year a friend goes out of their way to call me, make me feel good, cheer me up, spend time with me, buy me a gift, that's as good as a Birthday, in fact, maybe even better. If we did this throughout the year, instead of on just one day, we would have more days of celebration, and any given day could be a Holiday. That's how I saw it, and in some ways, still do.

We don't have to pretend it is our Birthday or a Holiday, per se, but we can make a point of celebrating. See, in some ways, I think my ideas were very much Ciccina-like, and yet in some ways, the ideas were not jelled and just weren't coming together, yet. On one level, maybe I had the right idea, but it wasn't thought out enough or maybe my execution was off? I also didn't have much opportunity to explore or vet out the possibilities. I felt like I didn't have much leeway because so many of my ideas were so far from the norm that I didn't have people around me who would go along with them. I didn't bother to explore too much further for fear of alienating myself more from my circle of friends, family and acquaintances.

In fact, I had alienated enough people in my life just deciding not to do the gift-giving thing on Christmas just because it was Christmas, for example. This used to drive some people I knew, crazy. To me, gifts were meaningless when given or received just because it was a Holiday designated as the gift-giving Holiday. It's not that I didn't like receiving gifts, or giving gifts, quite the contrary, but I rather liked giving gifts just because, better than because I was forced to do it. I enjoyed giving gifts when people least expected them, for no apparent reason other than, "I was thinking of you." To me that was even more special. Anyone could give a gift at Christmas, but how many people gifted, just because?

It was a concept, that every time it came up in conversation, needed explaining. And it was one which people either totally got, or totally hated. I suppose I had been on the path of exploring lots of different concepts outside the norm. Some of the concepts weren't well developed, decidedly. Some of these concepts were in need of improvement. And some of them might have even been right, but I just was going through the motions, clumsily, until I could figure it out and piece it all together.

I certainly never had a role model for this way of living or thinking.

It was definitely outside of the box, but I wondered if it was more of the way most of us would rather live than not. Some of these concepts, ideas, ways of being, ways of living, etc., felt so radical, but once I really started to understand them and incorporate them, they felt like an old shoe and felt like the "right" way, for me, at least. I had just been conditioned for so long to do it the "wrong" way, let's say, that to do it the "right" way seemed wrong. Since I obviously wanted a role model, Ciccina proved to be the best role model, ever.

Ciccina's Christmas gifts were the way she greeted me every single morning, or after not seeing me for an hour. Ciccina's Birthday Gifts were her kisses and lap sitting and pawing at the most appropriate times and unexpected times. Ciccina was the funniest Valentine of all with her Valentine gifts being the funny things she did that made me laugh, giving a whole new meaning to the song "My Funny Valentine." After all, laughter is the best medicine, right, so maybe it's the best gift too?

I remember reading once, that if newborn babies are not touched lovingly, they could die. I wonder if we retain that as adults? So, between the touching and the laughing, Ciccina's gifts ranked right up there for me, year round, 24/7. Of course one could argue that Ciccina is a dog, and a dog does what a dog does. People have responsibilities and families, and jobs, etc., so they cannot be around 24/7 to do for us what dogs do.

However, how often do we call people just to call them? How often do we speak to the little ones, the children, in our lives? The children, that's a good one. There are friends, aunts and uncles, and sometimes even absent parents who don't talk to the children in their lives or not in their lives all year. But come Christmas, they have to "let them know that they are loved," by sending them or giving them something in a wrapped up box. We "love" some people and some children so much, that we will fight crowds in stores, pay high retail prices, waste a lot of natural resources in paper wrappings and ribbons, fight long lines at the post office to put boxes in boxes and send things across the world to them, but we can't call them "out of the blue," to say, "thinking of you," or "I love you," on any given day?

When I would share this philosophy with friends and family, they would disagree and say I was the bad one for not sending a gift? This was not the case with all friends and family. My brother and sister-in-law tried to teach me this very concept on various Holidays, and even though I wanted to get it, I still wasn't getting it. That's how ingrained this was in my psyche.

I visited my nieces and nephews as often as I could and definitely called on their Birthdays and Holidays and yet I still felt like I had to, or wanted to give a material gift. I remember asking my sister-in-law, what I could buy the kids for Christmas, and she literally said, "Put a leaf in a box and tell them after they open up the gift, you will spend time with them leaf hunting." She went on to say, "That's the best gift you can give them, spend time with them, that's really what they want."

At the time, I just wasn't having any of that. "That's all good and fine," I thought, "but the kids have to open a "real" gift under the tree, it's Christmas!" What did I mean by a "real" gift? In retrospect, I was thinking something big and plastic and cut out of a mold that everyone else might be getting that particular Christmas so they would say, "hey my Uncle got me a this," whatever "this" was "important" to the material world at the time.

Arghhh! I was so confused at that time. On some level I knew I had to do things differently and it would be right to do so, and on some level I couldn't. On some level I knew I already did things differently, but on another level I wasn't sure if the things I was doing were right for anyone, and sometimes, if they were even right for me. No one seemed to understand me, not even me. Interestingly enough, Ciccina never seemed to have a problem understanding me, or appreciating me. Of course, it's because she is a dog, but at the same time, I was thinking that there was something else happening, a realization, or an awakening of sorts.

Sometimes the pendulum has to swing in order to reach equilibrium. Sometimes we have to break molds in order to make new ones, break habits, break tradition, etc. I knew this was what was happening, and I knew it wasn't supposed to feel comfortable, or at least it usually does not, but I felt damned if I did and damned if I didn't.

Back to Ciccina, I wasn't trying to "romanticize" the Ciccina story, but it seemed like everyone else was. I knew the kind of comments that people normally said about dogs, like she's so cute, or, he's so sweet, or, she's so cuddly, etc. But in Ciccina's case, what I got repeatedly was "She's so happy." When I would proceed to explain to them that this was a temporary "arrangement," they would laugh and say the usual, "She is so your dog." I never saw Ciccina as "my" dog, if anything, I saw her as my teacher. But dog or teacher, everyone thought she was happy.

I found this "happy" thing very curious. In analyzing it, she wasn't always happy. I saw her with certain people and in certain situations that showed me she was definitely not happy in those moments, or situations. That proved to me that when she was happy around me, which was usually always, she was genuinely happy. As much as little things bothered me, she didn't seem to be bothered too much that I hadn't figured out how to change the gift-giving thing or the Birthday thing, or when to celebrate Holidays thing.

Of course, she was a dog, and those things meant nothing to her anyway. Which gave me even more reason to ponder as to how they had become such a big thing for us humans, mandatory, obligatory things, at that. And for that matter, it was not only mandatory that we celebrate a given Holiday, and give a gift on a given Holiday, but that we be present and be "Happy," on that Holiday. Perhaps the most interesting thing of all was, the way I saw it, was that "you're supposed to be 'happy', because it is Christmas," kind of thing, was actually causing more problems for a lot of people. People who didn't have enough money to buy gifts, or had just been fired or were not in good relationships, were either over spending or over pretending, and/or feeling guilty, and thus only worsening the situation for all involved.

In the meantime, I had to still live my "people" life, and speaking of Holiday's, that particular day was the Fourth of July, and I had to still experience it in the best way I knew how. For the time being, I had decided to experience it by staying home and working, aside from making a few phone calls and sharing Holiday greetings with a few friends and family, as I said, on the phone.

While making my calls, there was one of my friends I wasn't able to reach and for some reason, I felt strongly about wanting to connect with him on that particular day. I had heard that he and his family had gone off to some mountain cabin to spend time away from civilization and probably didn't have cellular reception. That could very well have been the case, but for some reason, knowing that did not stop me from trying to reach him several times that morning.

I left several messages after each call and perhaps because of that, in the early afternoon, I heard from him. He sounded a bit disturbed, and I asked him what was going on to make him sound like that. He began to tell me that that very morning, his daughter tripped while she was running around playing and hit her lip on a fence, or something, and consequently cut a large gash on her face that had bled profusely.

He said that he and his wife recognized immediately that it was something that would require stitches. Besides the normal parent worries of facial scarring and pain and all that, they were several hours from the nearest hospital, or clinic, and were concerned about further complications. To make matters worse, their daughter did not want her parents to attend to the wound and wanted to be left alone.

He went on to say that at the moment his daughter hit her lip, of course, she yelled out a loud, painful cry. Evidently, her Mother went into hysterics and started screaming louder than her daughter and rushed over to her wanting to see what happened, while going through the "usual," Motherly type reactions, many of us are "understandably" accustomed to experiencing. I write "usual," because, maybe this too is something we have been taught. Maybe this is not inherent to who we truly are, but has become normal to who we have become or have been taught to be or how we have been "taught" to react to certain situations.

When my friend's wife started doing this, their daughter, evidently, immediately stopped crying in reaction to her Mother's histrionics, and wanted to get away from her. Both my friend and his wife, being very attentive parents, insisted that they be able to see what had happened and pulled their daughter's hands away from her mouth to see what the wound was like to determine how best to attend to it.

It was obvious to them that the wound was big because they could see an open gash and because blood was gushing out. Their daughter evidently pried herself away from them, and at her adamant insistence; they agreed to give her a moment to herself. This would also allow them time to calmly try and figure out what best to do under the circumstances, and for their daughter to have a moment to herself as well. My friend made a point of telling me that there was something very poignant in the way their daughter looked at her Mother and the way she instantly stopped crying that caused him to pause and take note that something different was going on rather than the "usual" child/accident behavior.

I said to him that perhaps she was trying to show her Mother that this way of being was not serving anybody and the situation, and that there was another way that could serve them all better? He said that it was interesting that I should say that because while their daughter went off to a corner somewhere, he and his wife devised a plan of getting to a hospital right away. In the meantime, they had gotten a wet rag and some medical supplies to go tend to their daughter's wound.

My friend went on to say that they could not have been prepared for what they saw when they returned to their daughter and removed her hands from her mouth once again, this time to clean the blood and the wound. He said, in his carefully chosen words, that the gash had been reduced to not much more than a scratch. He went on to say that the "scratch" had stopped bleeding and was on it's way to healing.

My friend, having studied Pre-Med at the University level, and having worked in a hospital for many years, in an emergency room, no less, knew the difference between a gash and a scratch and he said, he had never seen anything like that happen ever before. After taking a moment to take it all in, I said, "Wow, she is miraculous," referring to his daughter. "I knew it," I went on to exclaim, "she wanted to get away from her Mother who was exhibiting the old paradigm of worry, drama, trauma, and eventually the thought of old healing patterns, and wanted to show us all a new way." My friend had to agree and said that they had gotten that lesson too and something that had been quite a scare had ended up being such a learning experience.

My heart went out to all of them for having to have experienced the trauma, especially knowing they were so far from a medical facility and on a Holiday no less. I was also so proud of them for really getting what it might have actually been all about. "Maybe it happened just to teach us all this?" I heard myself say to my friend. We both hoped that we wouldn't have to learn lessons that way, the hard way, again, and that we would learn our future lessons through joy and fun, instead.

Was it a coincidence that I really felt like I needed to speak with this particular friend and that I evidently was calling him at the exact time all of that was happening? Upon hanging up the phone, I could no longer sit still, I had to tell everyone this miraculous story and wanted to share it with as many people as I knew. I wanted to tell them about this new paradigm of healing, something about self-healing, even though I wasn't quite sure exactly how or what it was.

The desire of wanting to share this experience with friends reminded me that I had an opportunity to share with friends on that very day, but I had turned it down. If I accepted the invitations, I also had the possibility to experience the joy by being and potentially learning through joy that I had been referring to moments before on the phone. Was turning down these kinds of invitations part of my old paradigm of how I thought I was supposed to do things? Were there maybe going to be lessons I could learn through joy and fun with my friends instead of having to learn through "working" by myself on this particular day?

I decided that though the day was half over, that there was still half a day left at this point, and I would live that half a day to its fullest. Having gotten the lesson and analogy, I decided that I would not just go to one party, but that I would still have time to go to at least two parties. I called two hosts for starters and asked them if I could still come to their parties. I felt like Ebenezer Scrooge in "A Christmas Carol," when he found out that he hadn't missed Christmas after all. My friends said, yes, come, and they both said it would be okay if I brought Ciccina. I hadn't missed the Fourth of July, and Ciccina and I were about to go celebrate this day together and with good friends.

17 DOGS JUST WANT TO HAVE FUN

"Ciccina, bye-bye?" That's all she had to hear, "We're going to a party," I added, as if she understood or as if it mattered. Everything was a party to Ciccina, as long as we were spending time together. Fourth, Fifth, Six, or any day of July, life to her was one big party. And that very day she was reminding me to live just for the sake of living, be just for the sake of being, and lest I forgot, in my opinion, the whole reason for the season of her being in my life, "love just for the sake of loving."

First party was my friend Laura's party. I was really glad I had decided to go to her party. Laura threw great parties, and that particular party was going to be the first party she threw since she had lost her dogs, Nicky and Andy. I knew it wasn't going to be the same without them there, and I hoped, in some way, that Ciccina would be able to help bring pet dog energy to the party.

Upon arriving at the party, Laura was as magnanimous as always to Ciccina and after greeting me she took Ciccina in her arms and walked her around introducing her to her guests. She introduced her as "Filippo's dog, but not his dog," and briefly told people the story. Her story ended with, "We are looking for the right home for her." "Right Ciccina?" she turned to her to say, "We're gonna find you the pewfect home with the besht famiry!" She said in her baby/puppy talk, and then they kissed each other very lovingly.

After the grand introduction to her guests, Laura took Ciccina into the kitchen where she had prepared for her a meal fit for a doggy Princess. As she put the finishing touches on Ciccina's feast, she told me how she just knew Ciccina and I were going to be coming, so she had prepared something special for her like she used to prepare for Nicky and Andy at parties like that one.

When I thanked her and told her she shouldn't have, she told me that she did it for Ciccina, because she's special. Yes, she was and after feasting on her meal, Ciccina joined all of Laura's guests and became the "Belle" of the ball. She got so much loving attention from all of Laura's friends at the party. Laura was like a Mother cub, watching the whole time to make sure Ciccina was having fun and being treated right. Laura even stopped a guest from feeding Ciccina something that would not be good for her. She instructed the children how to pet Ciccina. That day, it seemed like Ciccina was more Laura's dog than mine. I knew Laura was an animal lover and even though I knew this, I still couldn't help but to think that she and Ciccina also had a special bond between them that I couldn't deny.

Laura always had a special way with animals. As much as I loved Ciccina, I thought I could never care for her as well as Laura could. Ciccina didn't seem to mind me not being like Laura, but she sure loved Laura being the way she was. Throughout the party, if Ciccina wasn't with me, she would be with Laura; if she wasn't with Laura, she would be with me. It was kind of funny actually; though lots of people showed her a lot of attention, she really only cared about the two of us. In fact, of all the people Ciccina had met, Laura was very special to her. As a rule, she liked all my friends, but Laura, for some reason was special to her, and vice versa.

It started to get late and knowing I had at least another party I wanted to go to before I called it a day, I started saying my goodbyes. Everyone was sorry to see the "Belle" of the ball leave the party. Many of the guests came to say good bye to her first, and then to me and proceeded to tell me how lucky I was to have her in my life, and didn't understand why I would want to give her away. I politely smiled and said, "I know, I am very lucky, and I'm going to miss her."

Before I got out the door, Laura took Ciccina up into her arms and gave her a whole bunch more kisses before she seemingly, regretfully handed her back over to me. "Take good care of her," she said to me, and off we went.

The next party we went to was at a friend of a friend's. My friend Peter invited me knowing it would be okay not only for me to attend but he had asked his friend if it was okay to bring a dog, and it was okay. He told me that the party was an outdoor pool party and that he would bring his dogs too, and knew it would be fine and fun for us all.

I had never really brought Ciccina to a party where there were other dogs. This was going to be interesting. I was enjoying this "going to a party just to go to a party" thing and I was glad not to be at home and working, and instead, having fun being out with my friends and Ciccina.

As I left Laura's I called ahead to let Peter know that we were on our way. When we got to the second party, my friend Peter greeted us at the gate. He said I could remove Ciccina's leash so she could run around and play. Just as I removed Ciccina's leash, four or five dogs rushed us. I say that the dogs rushed us, but the dogs didn't seem to notice me, they made a bee line for Ciccina. In fact, I came to learn later, just how much they had "noticed" her and how much attention they really were giving her or wanted to give her.

As the dogs quickly approached Ciccina, she darted to get away from them. In the blink of an eye all four or five dogs started chasing Ciccina across the yard. In her attempt to get away from them, and not knowing the lay of the yard, Ciccina landed herself directly into the swimming pool. This got everyone's attention and though she was swimming just fine, people rushed to her rescue, more to be heralded as the heroes of the "damsel in distress," than anything else.

In an instant, Ciccina had won the hearts of everyone at yet another party. All the other dogs stopped cold at the edge of the pool, while Ciccina was clearly stunned herself, but safe and treading water. Funny, when Ciccina was wet she looked like a completely different dog. In fact, she was small and cute to begin with but wet, she was tiny and the cutest thing, at least we all thought so.

Evidently the other dogs did too, because as soon as she was placed back on dry land, all the other dogs went running after her again, except one, and that one belonged to my friend Peter. I commented to Peter how well behaved his dog Nellie was, and he started laughing and reminded me that his dog was a female. It took me a moment to figure out what he meant by that comment.

I inferred from his comment that the other dogs were male. My eyes automatically looked to the dogs to verify that that was indeed the case. When I took a glance to verify if I could see their genitalia, I was shocked to see everyone of the other dogs were not only all males but were all in an excited state. I was the last one to notice and the last one to laugh. Everyone had been talking about it and laughing and I had been completely oblivious to it all up until that point.

My laughter was interrupted by a thought, "Oh no!" I thought, "That's my Ciccina these dogs are fantasizing about." I had never thought of how attractive other dogs might have found her. I never even considered the thought. I had no time to ponder it because I noticed that one of the dogs in particular was really trying to have his way with Ciccina. It was obvious Ciccina wasn't interested and was holding her own very well, especially considering the much larger size of the other dog. I knew I needed to protect Ciccina and much to the amusement of everyone there, I went chasing after her behind all the dogs like a scene out of an old cops and robbers silent film.

When I got close enough, I called out, "Ciccina," and she immediately ran towards me and up into my open arms she jumped, she and her soaking wet fur. Immediately after landing in my arms, safe and secure, she made herself comfortable and proceeded to shake herself like there was no tomorrow until most of the water was off of her and on me, my pants and my shirt.

Only when I was soaking wet did she settle down into my lap. She panted with exhaustion, and yet I felt she was beaming with satisfaction and contentment that I had come to her rescue once again. Incidentally, one would think that it would be no big deal me getting all wet from holding a wet dog since we were at a pool party. In fact, both of these parties were pool parties and most everyone had on their swimsuits. Me? I had on my hand woven raw silk shirt and cotton pressed pants and Gucci loafers like I was going to a Country Club or something. I don't recall what I was thinking when I got dressed for these parties. I had much to learn still.

The point being, that Ciccina had done it to me again, all over my clothes, and me, and before long she, in all her wetness, would be in my car too. Not only had I let her, I kind of wouldn't have had it any other way, at that point. I had to protect her from the horny dogs, and that was that. My how far I had come from our first night, in such a short time. Inside I had a good laugh at myself.

In fact, everyone was having a laugh. Ciccina and I were a sight to behold. I was soaking wet, and panting, Ciccina was soaking wet and panting, and all around us were four dogs panting, horny and tails wagging staring at her. Everyone was staring, too, at this whole scene that within a few minutes had become the happening at this party. Ciccina was yet again the "Belle" of the ball. As if I didn't attract enough attention on my own when I went out, I attract to myself a dog who got just as much if not more attention than I. Oh, the irony. Oh, the perfection.

The thought of Ciccina being a female dog and commanding that much attention of male dogs was all new to me. For all I knew it may have even been new to Ciccina who was visibly not interested in any of her "suitors." She was perfectly content sitting on my lap. And much like Laura was doing at the previous party, at this party, it was Peter who went around telling people the story of Ciccina and how we met and how she "wasn't my dog." I appreciated him throwing that into the story for my sake, even though I don't think he believed it himself. When he came back around to me, I asked him to help me handle the awkward situation we were in, that of the four dogs still gathered around us and still aroused, staring at Ciccina.

Peter thought the whole thing was funny, as did everyone else, but for my sake, he grabbed a bunch of balls, called the dogs away, and started playing with them. One by one the dogs cooled down and I was able to put Ciccina back down. At first she jumped right back into my lap, but as she saw that the coast was clear, she was happy being on the grass, only she was careful not to stray very far from me. That was fine with me, because I liked having her close.

As the evening got later and darker, I put Ciccina on her leash and kept her close by as we continued to "entertain" the other guests with more stories. By the time it was time for us to leave, it seems that everyone had come over to "pay their respects" to Ciccina, who was only too happy to oblige them with a few wags of the tail as they petted her and showed her affection.

The fireworks had come and gone and they could be seen from Peter's friend's house but I hardly paid attention and they were almost uneventful compared to all the activities we had experienced that day. They actually didn't seem to faze Ciccina at all either. Maybe they were far away enough that the noise wasn't that loud or maybe she was otherwise preoccupied or content just to be, and be safe at that.

What I did know, was that when it finally got dark, it was not only time to go, but time to call it a night. At that point it had gotten very late and we had had much fun, and it too late for any more partying and time to say our goodbyes. Once again the litany of "You two are too cute together," was the predominant partying comment. What was different at this particular party was the addition of the comments that sounded like, "I hadn't laughed that much in years... when she ran right into the pool...." It seemed that no matter where we went and what Ciccina and I did together, everyone had a story of the experience to add.

I was glad Ciccina and I had helped people "Be," "Live," "Laugh," and "Love," more today. For her, I was happy that she had had attention from all the people and her very own canine groupies too. For me, I was happy that I enjoyed being, just for the sake of being and that I got to enjoy my friends and in their words, "Live a little."

Ciccina and I both happily jumped into my car. I removed Ciccina's leash as I always did in the car and she, though still a bit damp, was free to roam about the car and me all over my lap. Off we went happily home after a successful night. This day had been very different than what I had originally planned for myself. This had been a good Fourth of July. I was glad and grateful I hadn't missed it.

18 THE NIGHT THAT CHANGED MY LIFE FOREVER

Ciccina and I arrived home like every other night that we had gone out in the months we had been together. I had gotten into the habit of leaving her leash off when arriving home, late at night because there was no one around and I felt she so loved leading the way and beating me up the stairs to the front gate. I would eventually make it up there and with her nose pressed up against the part of the gate that didn't open, she would wait for me to unlock the gate and dash in between the slightest opening to race me to the front door.

It had become like a game we played, and she always won, and not just because I let her win. On the rare occasion that we would run into someone, she would usually ignore them, probably because at this point she was as tired as I was and we both had bed on our minds. And so it went every night that we were out until late, like clockwork.

Tonight was no different. I left her leash off and she beat me to the first gate, the garage gate. I let her out of that gate and she raced up to the front gate, just like she always did. She met me at the top of the stairs and as I went to unlock the gate, I looked down to see her nose pressed up to the part of the gate that stayed stationary. Her nose wasn't there pressed up against the gate. Instead she was behind me not even looking at the gate but looking the other way, toward the street.

I had an uncomfortable feeling, like a bad premonition, so I put down the things I had in my hand so I could pick her up. All of a sudden I heard her bark as her gaze was fixed at something across the street. I looked up briefly to assess what might be going on and I noticed that someone was getting out of their parked car, something that happened all the time and something that never alarmed her before. But for some reason, at that time, this particular person attracted her and my attention. As I quickly leaned forward to pick her up I had a vision of her being run over on the same four lane street from which I had rescued her but a few months before. In that split second, I also somehow had time to argue with myself that it wouldn't be possible for her to be run over because except for that car that had parked the street, there weren't any other cars around.

This was one of those rare occasions when the street was not busy at all. It was the Fourth of July evening and around midnight at that, so there were no cars. Plus she never ran into the street, except that time when I rescued her when she was running across the street, so there would be no chance that she could be run over? All this ran through my head in a split second, as I lunged to pick her up, not wanting to take any chances.

Just as my hands started to clinch around her body, I felt her fur brush my hands as she bolted out from between them, down the stairs and right into the street. My heart jumped to my throat as I screamed out to her "CICCINA! CICCINA!!!!!" As if something had happened and before anything could have happened, almost as if I knew something was going to happen, I cried out loud, "Why is this happening?"

I started to run down the stairs. I was halfway down the steps when I heard what sounded like a car speeding down the street going much faster than the speed limit and at a speed that would normally not have been possible had it not been for the fact that there were and had been no cars in the road. "CICCINA!" I cried out, anticipating the worst. But it was too late. I heard two of the most horrible sounds I'd never wanted to hear. One was the sound of what looked like an SUV running over Ciccina at full speed without even knowing that it had done so. And the second was the dying, crying yelp of MY Dog, My Ciccina, My Teacher, My Friend, My Companion calling for My Help.

"Yelp, Yelp," came her feeble but heart wrenching cry. Immediately tears started streaming down my face, as I stood frozen for a moment that seemed like an eternity, on the sidewalk at the edge of the street exclaiming, "Why is this happening, God why?" This was on the same street that just a few months before I had been her rescuer, risking an accident myself, to cross the road to save her. This was the same street where I was worried for her safety as I watched her cross it with bated breath. At that point, on that very street, months later, she lay dying.

I couldn't help but think that I failed her, that it was my fault. My mind was full of self-blame, sadness, anger, and questions. "What am I supposed to do now? How could I help her now?" What can I do now? How do I help her now? She was a goner to be sure. There was no way any dog could survive being driven over by an SUV at full speed, especially a cute little innocent, precious and delicate doggy like my Ciccina. I was sure her cry was her body's dying last breaths.

"Yelp, yelp," she continued like a metronome. "Yelp, yelp," the disturbing sound of a life's last and final plea for help. An untimely plea for more time, like my cry to God as to why this had happened, and of all times, during my watch and before I could deliver her to a loving home and family. A life that was loved by so many people was over.

What was I going to say to my family? What was I going to say to my nieces who would get on the phone with me just to ask me about Ciccina and wonder when they would get to see her again? What would I say to my Mother, to my friends, and to Laura?

What would I say to Ciccina? And what would I say to God for letting this happen? This wasn't right, it wasn't supposed to be like this. In a week and a half, I would have turned Ciccina over to a new owner and they would have given her a new home, a new name, a whole new life, a life that she deserved. She didn't deserve to die and if it had been her time, then she didn't deserve to die like this! This was a horrible way to die. It just wasn't right. What would Dorothy have to say about this now? What was all this for? What good could this possibly serve? Certainly all lessons had come to an end.

These and more thoughts went through my head as what seemed like a million things were happening at the same time. The only thing that wasn't happening is that no more cars were going by. None! But that and nothing else seemed to matter because I felt that I had failed the one being that loved me unconditionally.

Not only did I feel it was my fault, but I also felt helpless to help her and hopeless for the whole situation. I had no idea what I would find when I approached her, but no matter what the condition of her body, I did not want her dying last breath and last yelp to be alone and in the street without me. I looked both ways before crossing the street by force of good habits, though it was not necessary since there were no cars to be seen or heard. I squeamishly and apologetically made my way almost completely to the other side, as I retraced her path to death's door.

I walked up to her not knowing if she would be dead before I got there and what I would find. I had seen many animals on the road in all my riding and driving experiences and could not stand the thought that one of those could be my Ciccina. What happens to all that joy, that love, that meaning, when an animal dies? How could all that happiness, all those experiences, all those learnings have been wrapped up in such a small and adorable package, and then how could it all disappear all of a sudden just because of an "accident?" It was a split second, a blink of an eye, a moment in time! How could one's whole world change so quickly? It wasn't fair, it wasn't right!

The yelping continued like a metronome, "yelp, (pause), yelp, (pause), yelp, (pause), yelp...," as if marking my every step all the way there. Arriving to her, as I looked down upon my precious bundle of love and fur, I saw her sprawled in ways dogs cannot normally and should not ever be sprawled. Her hind legs were completely apart, her body was twisted and her face was squashed sideways and it was bleeding all over the street. As bad as she looked, it did not seem like the weight of the whole SUV had been on top of her little body. Regardless of how she was hit it was life and death, and most certainly, death. I was heart-broken.

"Yelp, yelp." What was she trying to tell me with this haunting yelp? Was she telling me goodbye? Was she saying "Help me?" Was she saying, "Don't leave me. I need you right now, more than ever. Don't let me die alone!"

I wanted to tell her that I was so sorry I let this happen to her and that I loved her, but all that kept coming out of my mouth was the desperate plea, "Why is this happening? Why is this happening?" I needed meaning. I needed understanding. I needed help. In all of this time I had looked to Ciccina to teach me, help me learn and help me grow. I had looked at her as if she was the one that was tuned into what was right in certain moments. In that moment I needed to know things more than ever, but that moment, Ciccina needed me to know!

One thing I knew for sure was that I needed to get her out of the street for her sake and mine too. Again, in all this time, which was probably just another moment in time but seemed like a lifetime that I stood there in the street looking at her crushed and mangled body and pondering what to do. There were no cars, NO CARS! And whoever had gotten out of their parked car that had presumably gotten Ciccina's attention was no where in sight? In fact I wondered, didn't that person who got out of their parked car hear Ciccina bark? Did he hear me yell? Didn't he hear the car and the yelp and more of my yelling? Where was he? Where was anybody?

I felt so alone in a street normally full of cars and an area full of people. It was as if the town were deserted. Help or no help I had to pick up Ciccina but I didn't want to hurt her any more than she already was hurting. As far as I was concerned, I had hurt her enough and didn't want to cause her last moments any more pain than she already was experiencing.

I wanted so much to hold my Ciccina. I wanted to give her love and attention. I wanted to let her know that I was there for her and that I loved her even though I had failed her. I wanted her to know that I was sorry. I wanted to thank her for what she had meant to me and everything she had done with me and for me. But this wasn't the time, or maybe she already knew that, and obviously, in any case, this was the end of the road, so whether she knew it or not, it was too late. It made me think that I had to make a point of letting people know how much they meant to me when I had the opportunity because we just never know. Ah, and here was another lesson I was learning.

I leaned down to pick Ciccina up as I had wanted to only moments, or minutes before, at the gate, and had I done so, or had I been able to do so, none of that would have happened. If only I had been able to, we would have been on our way to lying, snuggly, in our respective beds by that point. Only at that point, Ciccina lay practically glued to the street in a pool of her own blood.

For me, that moment was one of the hardest moments of my life, so hard for me to take. Nonetheless, I summoned up the courage and amongst her methodical yelping I gathered her up and gently brought her bloodied broken body close to my chest and heart. I don't remember even giving a thought to the fact that the blood would ruin the shirt or the pants, none of that obviously mattered at that moment, or maybe, anymore. I didn't care, I knew what was important and what was important to me was the fact that I wanted Ciccina back.

I wanted things to go back to the way they were. I wanted her smiling and wagging her tail and I wanted her kisses. The same ones I didn't let her give me, even till that very night when she jumped into my arms and shook her wet self off after jumping in the pool. Though I never let her kiss me before, she never gave up trying and jumped up at that point to kiss me and I turned my head like every other time.

At the very least I wanted her to try do that to me again, only at that point, I would let have her kiss me. I would have let her, I really would have. Why did things have to change? I wasn't prepared for that change? Had I been prepared for any of the changes that had occurred during that whole time with Ciccina? Hadn't I become open to change during that time? This was one change I wasn't opened to.

The moment I held Ciccina in my arms, her yelping stopped. I was certain she had died and I cried all the more. I was glad that she at least knew I had been there for her at the end. I was also happy that she died in my arms instead of alone in the street. But my heart could not believe that she was dead, and didn't want to believe it. I looked at her, almost forgetting that I was still in the street as I slowly walked across the fateful lanes as if walking in a funeral processional. I stared at her the whole time and she stared, period. Ciccina's eyes were glued open and she did not blink at all. She was frozen, stiff, paralyzed. My Ciccina was dead in my arms.

I had never held a dead dog in my arms. For that matter, I had never held anything dead in my hand except a Goldfish, that I can recall. I would have expected her body to go limp. I would have expected her body to be cold. I didn't know how long this process was supposed to take, but for her sake I was hoping that it would happen quickly.

As I made it to the front gate, I had to awkwardly maneuver myself, while trying to hold her still, to unlock the gate and get it open. And I could tell that as I moved I was hurting her, and my blood sank further to my feet than it already had. I was hurting my Ciccina in her last moments.

Hurting her? Having had that thought indicated to me that she was not dead after all, or yet. And then at that very moment, just like I had had the premonition that she would run into the street and get run over, I had a premonition that "she's not going to die." "She's not going to die?" I screamed inside my head, "so now what do I do?"

In my mind I had to switch gears from making her comfortable as she died to helping her live. I was so excited and sad at the same time. I was excited that I was believing that Ciccina, for all intents and purposes, would come back from the dead. At the same time I had a hard time believing she really could live and if she did, that she could ever be like she was before. I thought to myself, how do Doctors fix squashed faces and crushed bodies? "Was my Ciccina ever going to be the same as she was before?" My mind raced with the thought of the pain she would have to endure in the hospital, in surgery, in casts, etc.

Nevertheless, I hopped into gear and quickly went into action to help my Ciccina live. "She's going to live," I heard in my head, and I kept repeating to myself, "She's going to live." "Now what do I do?" I opened the front door and turned on the lights. I grabbed a pillow from the couch and brought it into the office with me. I threw the pillow on the floor to lay her on. I thought that in case she moved at all, I didn't want her falling off a chair or something. I then placed her paralyzed, bloody body onto the pillow with her sad, squished, frozen, crooked face, facing my desk.

Her eyes were still stuck open and showed no signs of life and her lifeless, paralyzed body lay there completely helpless and motionless. Regardless, "She's going to live," I had heard in my head. "She's going to live," I repeated. "You're going to live!" I took the affirmation I was hearing in my head and started repeating it out loud to her. "You're going to live Ciccina, you're going to live, okay? You're going to live."

What was I to do at that point, I wondered? I had not had her long enough to need to get her any shots or checkups or anything like that. So I had not been, or even knew where a veterinarian or animal hospital was. I wasn't planning on having her as long as I had her, so I never looked into the nearest hospitals, etc. I didn't know any of these things and was at a complete loss, especially in my confused and emotionally distraught state.

I wasn't thinking straight, but I was doing the best I knew how, and I knew I needed to do more. The only thing that was coming to my mind at that moment was to call 911. I called 911 and waited on hold with the phone on speaker. At the same time, I turned on my computer to look up phone numbers of doctors or veterinary hospitals in the area.

During emergency times like that everything seems to happen so fast, unless you want them to happen fast. I thought my computer was too slow as it was, but during that moment, it seemed like it was taking my computer too long to boot up, and my dial-up internet connection, at the time, was taking an eternity to connect, not to mention 911 still hadn't answered. Of course 911 had not answered as it was the Fourth of July, probably one of the busiest days for them. And for animals? What about the animals? I had the feeling nothing would be open, and it was at that point, past midnight, no less.

Of all days for this to happen, the Fourth of July and after midnight. It was like the perfect storm. I couldn't think of anyone I could call at that time, and the one number I thought to call, and I thought could help, had me on hold. Once my computer finally booted up, I started looking up animal care, in the city where I lived, and was coming up short. I possibly wasn't using the correct words. I thought maybe I should try to type in "emergency," so I tried that.

"Why isn't 911 answering?" I was flustered, I was upset, I was doing all of this because a voice in my head said, "She is going to live," but I looked over at Ciccina and she was in the exact position she was when I placed her on the pillow on the floor. She had not moved, her eyes had not shut or blinked and I could not even see her breathing. It was arguable that she was even alive at that moment. Somehow I knew she was, I just knew she was.

In a moment of a little more clarity, I thought of the incident with my friend and his daughter just that morning. I reviewed the whole story in my mind of her showing them and all of us a new paradigm of healing and of living etc. I thought to myself, if my friend's daughter could do this, Ciccina can, because Ciccina can do things that I, or for that matter, most humans haven't tapped into, from what I could tell at the time.

Inspired by this story I turned and looked Ciccina directly in her eyes and I said to her out loud, "If you are supposed to live, I know you can heal yourself, I know you can and I know you can show me how. I will help you in any way I can but you gotta show me how. I believe in you, you can do it, you can do it, you can heal yourself. Do it Ciccina, do it, I'll help you. I love you!"

Having told her what I felt I needed to tell her, I turned back to my computer to continue looking for a clinic or some place I could take Ciccina where she could get the help I thought she so desperately needed in order to live. As I was doing this for the next couple of minutes, I turned to look at her for what seemed liked a million times. There was never a reaction, no change in her position, no blinking, no movement at all, just more bleeding onto the pillow.

In frustration, I gave up on waiting for 911 and hung up, and having temporarily distracted myself from the emergency at hand, I realized, that in my haste to get Ciccina indoors and get her help, I had left everything that I was carrying on the floor outside the gate. I had also left the front door open and all the lights on all over the place. I turned to Ciccina to say out loud, "I'll be right back Ciccina, I'll be right back," as I leaned down to pet her and let her know I was right there.

I was just going to go get my stuff from outside and to close the door and shut off some lights, but I didn't want her to think I was going out for long. Not that I thought she could hear me or understand me, but on some level I felt like I needed her to know and on some level I thought she could possibly know. In the process, I also thought it would give me an opportunity to clear my head so that I could come up with a new plan of action to get Ciccina the help that she so desperately needed if she was going to make it.

I went outside to get the stuff I had left behind. I came back inside and closed the door behind me. In my disturbed state I pushed the door too hard and it slammed. As soon as the door slammed and made a loud noise, I heard a yelp. Was it my imagination? The dog that had been laying motionless for all that time, suddenly yelped? It was not like the yelp I had heard on the street, this was a strong, loud yelp. The yelp was the kind of yelp that sounded like she had just been hurt. Had she tried to get up and realized that her legs were broken? Had she thought I had left when the door slammed and that I had forgotten her or left her all alone? Had the sound of the slamming door startled her? What had happened? "Ciccina?"

Whatever it was, I ran toward the office yelling all the way, "I'm here Ciccina, I'm here. I didn't leave you, I'm here." All the while I was feeling bad thinking that she might have thought I had abandoned her and left, slamming the door behind me. I didn't want her to feel alone during her time of need. I didn't know what was going on in her little mind but I was thinking the worst. I just didn't want her to suffer any more than she already had suffered.

As I ran toward her I yelled to her, "I'm here," so she could hear me from the other room until I got there, but with each yell on my part, she yelped all the more. This time her yelping wasn't methodical but it was non-stop, "yelp, yelp, yelp...," frenetically. I was feeling like she was in pain. The yelp was shrill and painful to listen to because it was coming from deep physical hurt, I could tell.

I yelled out all the more and all the while as I ran to her, but she didn't seem to hear me because she yelped all the more. I assumed she had lost her hearing in the accident and just couldn't hear me. I couldn't wait to be at her side so she could see that I was there, if she could still see. And if she couldn't see through her eyes stuck open, she could feel me, because I would pet her. Ciccina was definitely alive and soon I could pet her, caress her and console her so she would know for sure I was there and it was going to be okay. Filippo had not abandoned her.

19 RAISING HER VIBRATIONS

By the time I got to the office and looked at the pillow where I had laid Ciccina's body, and where she had lay frozen for awhile up until that point, she was gone. How could she have been gone? There was no way she could have walked? She was paralyzed, she was practically dead only minutes before, if not actually dead. What was going on?

Then I realized that I could still hear the yelping in pain and agony and in response to her yelping I yelled out, "I'm here, I'm here, I didn't leave you, I'm here." I wanted her to know I was there, in case she was looking for me and felt abandoned. As I yelled out, I was frantically running around the house looking for her everywhere, but she was nowhere to be found. Realizing that this was to no avail, I came to a halt and took a moment to breathe and collect my thoughts. I couldn't figure out what was going on. I was quiet long enough to hear yelping again. But it wasn't just yelping, she was making awful sounding noises and while yelling I could hear thumps as if she were bumping into things, followed by even louder yelps of even more agonizing pain.

What was going on? What had possessed her? Where was she and how did she get there, wherever she was? What was she doing and how was she doing what she was doing?

I started walking again. I walked into the hallway and started yelling out again, thinking she might be able to hear me better above her yelping and painful cries, "I'm here. Ciccina, I'm here. Where are you?"

All of a sudden I saw her! I was taken aback, like I had seen a ghost. In fact, she scurried herself past me so fast it was like a blur. It could have been my impression of it in the moment. I had such mixed emotions. On the one hand she was alive, for sure, on the other hand, there was so much wrong with what was happening, or was there? As she scurried by me, she was dragging her body behind her. Her back legs were not working. Apparently only her front legs were. How she could pull her weight with her front legs and so quickly and why was baffling me?

She was headed back into the office when she went by me, but not for long. I thought she was headed back to her pillow, but no, she shuffled by me again only this time into my bedroom. Then from my bedroom she shuffled past me again going toward the living room, then the dining room and the kitchen, out of my sight. It was time for me to be frozen. I couldn't believe what I was seeing. It was a horrific sight, like something out of a horror movie. Not that it scared me, but it was as if she had literally gone mad and had no idea what she was doing. It was like a chicken running around after its head had been cut off. It was painful to witness.

I snapped out of my bewilderment and tried to get her attention thinking that she had lost it and if I yelled louder I could get her attention and stop her from hurting herself even more. Whatever was happening was obviously very painful to her, unbelievably so, to be sure. I had never seen anything like it, I had never even heard or read anything like it and I didn't know what to think of it.

What made it worse was that while she pulled herself around and tried to scurry with her little legs, she was also evidently blind because she was bumping up against things. Either that, or she had no control, to be sure, and couldn't stop herself from bumping and maneuvering around walls, mirrored doors, furniture and all. She bumped into my bedroom mirrored closet door, and yelped very loudly. Then she bumped into the mirrored closet door in the office and yelped louder still. She ran into the living room and literally ran into the wall and yelped all the louder.

It wasn't as if she wasn't familiar with the lay of the place. And while yelling for her to be able to hear me and know I was there, I at the same time tried to wrap my mind around what was happening to her at this moment? I couldn't figure it out, nothing about what was happening made sense to me, and in my hyper state of awareness it was intensely horrifying. She showed no signs of stopping for any reason or for anything, least of all a wall or a mirrored door.

I felt helpless, like there was nothing I could possibly do. I had no frame of reference for this and I couldn't even grab her to stop her. I wasn't even sure if I wanted to or if I even should because I didn't want to hurt her. I wasn't sure she would even stop doing what she was doing even if I would be holding her, but a couple times, I tried to grab her, nonetheless. Her movements were so unpredictable and fast, I could not get her. Either that, or in my heart of hearts I didn't want to grab her. Something was happening and I wasn't sure what, and I wasn't sure anymore if it was bad or good, on top of the bad that had already happened. It was so confusing.

In the midst of my incessant thoughts, Ciccina, who had not stopped for a second, with a loud bang, ran into the sliding glass door. I was shaken to my core, my body tense from the pain that I felt she must have felt. But Ciccina kept on going. I yelled out in desperation, "CICCINA, CICCINA, I'm here," still thinking that she had gone mad over the fact that I slammed the door, which might have made her think I had left her.

And while I was yelling, I heard the voice again. I don't remember if it was actually a voice or if it was a "knowing," like a message in my head. All I know is that somehow the knowledge came to me that she was taking me at my word. The knowing information was that Ciccina was healing herself just like I had told her she could and she was showing me how. I remember having the question, " How she could possibly heal herself and how could this pathetic madness possibly be healing her?" At the same time that I had the question, the answer also came.

The answer was, that Ciccina was "Raising her vibrations." "Raising her vibrations?" I wondered. "Raising her vibrations," was the answer that repeated in my head.

All of a sudden it clicked and I felt 100% certain that she was definitely healing herself by raising her vibration. Even though I didn't know exactly what that meant, I knew for certain that this is what she was doing. I recalled my words to her that I would help her, but it was she who had to heal herself. I wanted to do something, but I didn't even know what was going on much less what to do, except for the fact that I knew SOMETHING BIG was happening in this moment and I needed to be present and listen for more answers.

I had never thought about healing in this way, nor did I understand it. And "raising her vibrations?" I couldn't even imagine what that meant in terms of healing. I was asking myself, "How can she do that?" That question turned to, "How was she doing that?" And then another question came to me, "What will it do exactly?"

These were all good questions, and they fascinated me, if they proved to be true. However, I felt that I was supposed to be part of this and asked the question, what can I do to help her? I knew I had to, and wanted to help her and the only thing I could think of was if she were raising her vibrations, maybe if I raised my vibrations too, I could somehow support her state? I wasn't even sure what I was telling myself. It didn't make sense in my mind, but somewhere in me, it made every bit of sense and I knew exactly what was going on.

I didn't know how to raise my vibrations, or at least never thought about it in this way, but I instinctively, or just as crazily as Ciccina, I started to jump up and down in place. I matched her mad, frenetic energy and jumped and jumped and jumped. While jumping I remembered hearing or learning or reading that the highest vibration in the Universe and the fastest speed something could travel was "Love." So, I concluded that if Ciccina was trying to raise her vibration and if the highest and fastest vibration was Love, I somehow had to give her or send her love.

I was already loving her and the only other thing I could think of doing while I was jumping was to send her love, in my mind and verbally, out loud. I proceeded to cheer her on, "I love you, I send you love, you are love, love, Ciccina, love, love, love, Ciccina love..." I cheered and cheered, love, love, love while tears streamed down my face by the bucket. I think I must have been crying for many reasons. Number one, she was still dragging her broken back legs all over the place and hitting her poor broken body up against everything, the walls, the doors, the piano, the couch... you name it, she hit it. That had to have hurt on top of the trauma her body already had endured.

I was also crying because I wanted her to do it, do something, do anything, raise her vibrations, and heal herself! If this was supposed to help her heal, then I wanted this so much for her. In other words, they were also tears of excitement, though I wouldn't go so far as saying tears of joy. I hadn't recalled ever feeling both of those so strong and crying for two extreme opposite reasons.

Adding to that, I was well aware that I was also crying because I didn't know what she was doing or for that matter what I was doing. I was confused and frustrated as to what was going on. At the same time, I think I might have been crying because I felt that there was a possibility she/we might be doing something so amazing, so miraculous, and that I was participating in a miracle occurring right in front of my eyes.

During a period of time which felt again like hours but was probably several minutes, and while I jumped myself to more and more exhaustion, in the craziness of my body movements, there came a stillness in my mind or in my consciousness. Ciccina continued to yelp for life and scurry and drag herself and hit against things while going through her process, whatever it was. In the stillness amidst the chaos of my mind, I heard, or thought, of other "healing" or "loving" words and phrases that I thought needed to be included in that moment.

My cheer, which consisted mainly of the word "love", started to include hope and encouragement that went something like this, "I know you can do this, Ciccina, I know you can heal yourself. Raise your vibration, raise it. Raise your vibration, you can do this. You can heal, I believe in you, I have faith in you. Heal Ciccina, heal. Show me how, I will help you."

In the stillness came the recollection about visualizations. I had read somewhere that some animal trainers visualized what they wanted the animal that was being trained to do, doing it in their mind. Some authors who wrote about these trainers went so far as to say that the animals, even wild animals, could see the images from the trainer's mind telepathically. I thought to include this too, along with my jumping and cheering. As I jumped and shouted out cheers, I started visualizing her as if she were running around from room to room in perfect physical health, wellness and happiness.

In my jumping frenzy, I still had my eyes on her every move, when she was in the same room as me. I kept jumping in the same place, in the living room, and she moved herself, somehow, from room to room, bouncing off of everything in each and every room. At yet another pivotal moment, I was able to notice that she was actually using her hind legs ever so slightly. At first I wasn't sure if I believed my eyes. It was ever so subtle. A little bit every once in awhile, although decidedly not effectively.

Use of her hind legs or not and though most surely in excruciating pain, Ciccina was not stopping, and my mind was starting to wrap around the idea that she was definitely going through some fantastical process. I couldn't imagine how she was keeping up her pace, especially with only the use of her front legs and dragging her weight. I was beginning to exhaust myself trying to, and quite possibly, or most definitely "raising my vibration" in support of her.

All of a sudden I heard a strange sound that took me out of the trance like state that I was in. It was way past midnight by now and I couldn't figure it was the phone ringing. I couldn't imagine who could be calling me at this time. Although there was a time when I used to have friends that I spoke to at all hours of the night, those times were long gone, and no one called me nor did I call anyone after ten. But it actually was the phone ringing. And as I stood there, it rang and rang.

Since my home phone was also a business line, I rarely answered it after office hours. People in different Time Zones would leave business messages and at various hours, but usually early morning, like East Coast Time, but not after midnight. Though for some reason, when I finally came to and when I finally realized it was the phone, I knew I had to answer it.

I stopped what I was doing, and it was perfect timing, because I don't know if I could have continued for much longer than I had. I thought I was in good shape, but I had never exerted my body in this frenetic way. Without even checking Caller ID, I picked up the phone, with certainty that I had to answer. I answered it with great anticipation, and got yet another surprise. It was my friend Marco. The surprise was that Marco, of all people, never called me late at night. Never. And never means never. In fact, Marco, as a rule, went to bed much earlier than I did, and much earlier than Midnight, that was for sure.

This call was an anomaly, and of all the times for him to call, here he was, right now in the middle of possibly one of the most tragic moments of my life, or possibly the moment of the biggest miracle I had ever participated in co-creating, or the biggest madness. I was feeling both at the same time and my friend was calling me.

In a voice which must have sounded very much unlike my own, and very much out of breath, I asked him why he was calling at this hour, and wondered if everything was okay with him. He responded by telling me he was fine but that he felt like something was going on with me and that he needed to make contact with me.

Wow, was this really happening? Did he really just say that? Who says that? Who does that? How did he know?

I had exhausted myself from jumping up and down on the hardwood floor in the living room and on top of it, I was emotionally drained, so the call from Marco was more than welcomed. I was so relieved to have the opportunity to talk to not just another human being, but a dear friend about what had happened, what was going on, and to contemplate what will happen. Probably, not coincidentally, Marco, of all people, was one of the people who was interested in the esoteric energetic healings and such and whom I would be able to talk to about what was happening. I knew whatever I told him about what had happened or what was happening, he wouldn't think it was weirder than I already thought it was.

While Ciccina continued yelping and hitting up against things all over my place, I practically collapsed on the floor of my kitchen where I had answered the phone. I crossed my legs and leaned my back on the cabinets behind me to take a breath and a moment to share with him what was happening.

Though I had phones in every room, I had purposefully taken the call in the kitchen so as to not disturb Ciccina and her process, since it was the room where she didn't drag herself into as much as the others. There was no stopping her, and I didn't want to stop her. I didn't plan on being on the phone very long anyway, because I wanted to be there for her and let her know I was present. But this moment with Marco on the phone was not only welcomed it seemed like it was divine timing, so I had to acknowledge it and talk to him. I had felt so alone in this process and didn't want to wake up any of my friends. I could have used someone to share this moment with and I didn't want to wake anyone up. Instead, someone I knew and loved, and who knew and loved me, called me after midnight, out of the blue.

"Marco," I started in, "You won't believe what happened tonight." I didn't go into too much detail; I wanted to get back to jumping up and down and sending Ciccina love and energy to help her with the raising of her vibrations.

It was interesting to me that I had no idea what that was or what that did, but because of that information that I heard or just knew, and because of the connection that I had made with my friend's daughter and her accident and subsequent healing that very morning, I knew it was right. There was something at work here that was beyond our normal human abilities, very similar to my friend's daughter.

It couldn't have been a coincidence that I had thought about my friend all day and called him over and over again until he finally responded and told me about his daughter's accident and eventual "strange," miraculous healing. It couldn't have been a coincidence that I told him that she was showing us a new way. Here was a new way. Well, at least a way that was new to me. For all I knew these ways were part of our given human abilities, and birth rights, but we just don't know about them? Or at least, I didn't know about them.

I told Marco what had happened. He couldn't believe it. Ciccina had been a dog he had immediately taken a liking to when he first met her. Marco enjoyed playing with her every time we had been together and Ciccina enjoyed him. She had already become family to him as well, even though I kept telling him that I was not going to be able to keep her and that I was looking for a good home for her.

I shed more tears as I shared the story with Marco and while simultaneously continuing to send love mentally to Ciccina and visualize her as healed. While on the phone with Marco, all of a sudden all the yelping and the noises and the shuffling and dragging and bumping up against things stopped. Every sound stopped all of a sudden. The silence was deafening and eerie to me. I couldn't imagine what could have happened.

I held my breath. What happened? Where was Ciccina? What did she do? Did she die?

With baited breath I said, "Marco, wait, something just happened." I put the phone down on the kitchen floor and was about to get up, when all of a sudden I see Ciccina's face appear from around the corner of the dining room wall. She peered around it as she walked toward me, ON ALL FOURS. She walked as if she were in a trance. I looked at her in awe and disbelief, like as if I was seeing a ghost, or better yet, a being, literally coming back from the dead.

This was obviously the dog that had just gotten run over by an SUV because her face was still smashed, but otherwise, if I didn't know what I knew, I wouldn't know it from looking at her walking toward me. She was exhausted and yet she wasn't panting heavily, which was unbelievable to me. I sat there on the floor of my kitchen, dumbfounded. I didn't know what to do or say. I had never heard of anything like this happening with anybody or any animal, ever. I had no point of reference for this kind of experience. I had forgotten Marco was still on the phone. I had no idea where I was or what was happening.

Again, it was almost as if the ghost of Ciccina was what was walking toward me. You know how when you watch television and you see people in an accident get mutilated, and then the ghosts, or spirit of the person gets up and walks normally? This is what Ciccina was doing. As if her body were in the living room somewhere and her spirit was walking toward me, like a zombie. But somehow more beautiful than a zombie, despite her crooked and bloody face. There was an air or an aura of peace, fulfillment, love. I couldn't explain it. She walked on all fours toward me all the while, staring directly into my eyes. My eyes locked with hers, and I watched her and I looked at her intently.

What was she saying? What had she done? What was going on?

Ciccina not only walked toward me, she actually lifted her front paws up one by one and landed them on my lap and she did the same with her back legs... up and... then she literally collapsed on my crossed legs.

I looked at her on my lap and I was dumfounded. I immediately gently put my hand on her withered body that lay on my lap, and gently caressed her in somewhat of a daze, being careful not to hurt her. I then remembered Marco was on the phone and I grabbed it and said, "Oh My God, Marco, you won't believe what just happened," I heard myself say again. Both of us in disbelief, me telling him and him hearing me, it was amazing what I was witnessing and what we all were experiencing.

"Raising her vibrations, Marco, that's what I heard, that she was raising her vibrations, can you believe this?"

"Marco, I gotta go," I said to him, as I knew I wanted to return all my attention and energy to Ciccina and try to decide what we needed to, or could do from that point. "Play her 'Dog Dreams,'" he said to me, "Play her the CDs, it will help you in your work," he continued. "What work," I asked. "In your healing work with Ciccina. That's your job, you're healing her, and the music will support that," he responded confidently.

Marco was referring to a series of CDs he had recently completed of his own musical compositions. He had gifted me the whole set, which was made up of two CDs for dogs, two for cats and one for horses. I had heard the music before many times. Though the CD set was conceptualized for animals, it was very much people music too and I did enjoy listening to them.

I did remember noticing that when I played Marco's music on occasion on the stereo, it was music that brought Ciccina into the room where the stereo was playing, as opposed to some music that made her leave the room if she had been in it. "It will help her with raising her vibrations, that's what my music does," Marco continued before hanging up. "Maybe he's right?" I thought at first. "Of course he's right," I said to myself, decidedly, "It is no coincidence that he called me on this very evening at this precise moment to give me a message."

I had stopped believing in coincidences a while back. I felt like everything that happened was for a reason. I felt that to my core, and yet, I also fought that in almost every aspect of my life. Signs, teachers, lessons, answers were everywhere, but I was not having any of it. The whole experience with Ciccina from the moment I decided to go buy munchies and came upon her was a great example.

Marco had called because he felt me and knew I needed someone to talk to. He also had a message for me, and that message was very clear, it was to play Ciccina the music to help her "raise her vibrations." He used my words, but they weren't my words, they came to me. Incidentally, these were the same words he used about his music. Coincidence? I don't think so. And then he said, "That's your job, you're healing her!" Those words echoed in my head and at the same time, resonated, because that is what this whole evening had been about since the "accident."

As I hung up the phone and placed it on the floor next to me, I didn't dare move an inch. I did not want Ciccina to have to move. The hand that was initially petting her, started to hover. No, it didn't just all of a sudden start levitating. What I mean by that is that my hand, "on its own", without my thinking I was going to do it, came off her body. It's not that I didn't will it, it had to have been like an unconscious thing, because it wasn't a thing I did. I am sure I had seen others do it, but it wasn't me. Nonetheless, I allowed my hand to hover over her body and just watched it and myself, and Ciccina, in the process.

Something was happening while my hand was hovering but I was not sure what, and I was not familiar with what was going on. Again, I had no frame of reference. I later learned, that this was commonly done by energetic healers but to me, I was just going with what was flowing and something was flowing and I let it flow.

Of course, I had control over my hand, but it didn't necessarily feel like I did. For a long while, I just held my hand steady a few inches above her body. What I was sensing or imagining, was that energy was coming out of my hand and going onto/into her. How did I know this? Where did this knowledge come from? How could I sense this?

There I stayed, again, for what seemed like hours with my hand hovering over Ciccina's body. All the while I kept thinking that this was also helping "raise her vibrations." I had this feeling or more appropriately, knowing, that something very special was happening and that Ciccina knew it too and was taking it all in.

I don't remember for how long I did this and how long we sat there. Again, I remember coming out of a daze, or a trance like state at one point and noticing that it was really late and wondering where the time had gone. Everything that had happened at that point was all a blur but one thing I knew for sure, a few hours before, I had a dead dog in my arms and hours later, I had a live one on my lap. That much I knew. What sort of condition she was in, I didn't know, but something was assuring me that she was on her way to normal again? Though this seemed highly doubtful at the time.

In my trance like state, or maybe it was a sleepy state, I remember thinking I was talking to Ciccina. I don't remember if I actually said anything out loud or not. Having been sure she had sustained internal injuries and bone injuries, I was very concerned again about her bodily state and my mind brought up the need to take her to be checked out again. I remember having a dialogue with Ciccina. She said, or someone did, or my mind was playing tricks on me, "We can do this, you and I, you will see."

As if I didn't understand anything of what I was hearing, I asked just to make sure, "Should I take you to a hospital?" Not that I had found a hospital yet, and at the later hour that it had become, if one had been open earlier, it certainly wouldn't have been anymore. I also wasn't just thinking for that moment, I was thinking I could take her to a hospital, period, if not at that point, then first thing in the morning. The answer that came back, again, surprised me. "No," came the answer.

Ciccina had been calling all the shots as far as I could tell, from the moment I looked into her eyes and said, that she could heal herself and I could help her. Who knows if she had been thinking the same thing before that point, or if this was her call to action from someone who knew her and loved her.

Regardless, there she was in my lap having done all that she had done to get herself to that point, telling me not to take her to the hospital, and that she was going to show me. Show me what? I felt responsible for Ciccina and one part of me felt I knew better. But it wasn't until she revived herself that I had ever seen the likes of what she did in "raising her vibrations," and healing herself enough to walk on all fours, albeit with a smashed face, and who knew what else might have been going on with her and inside her.

Wanting to make sure I was doing the right thing, I insisted. I continued my questioning to her in my mind, or to who knows what, saying, "But are you going to be okay?" "Yes, but we have to work," I heard in response. There it was again, "Work."What is this "work?" The answer didn't immediately come and I let it go for the moment, still arguing the point about getting her help. I was very concerned about her making it through the night, and persisted my questioning, "But are you going to be okay through the night?" In response, I distinctly heard, "Yes!"

I honestly did not know what was going on, or to whom I was talking. For all I knew I was talking to myself. And even at that, I didn't recognize myself to even understand which self I was having a conversation with. I had never said to anyone, or thought of saying to anyone, "You can heal yourself, I know you can, and I can help you." First of all, how would I know that with so much certainty? Secondly, what sort of help did I think I was proposing at the time?

I was grasping for things that I could know with certainty because there was so much that I didn't understand and so much that I wasn't sure of and so much that was new to me happening all at the same time. I wanted so much to understand and do the right thing based on my best educated guess, but everything that I was educated on seem to fly out the window in one evening and things I knew nothing about seemed to start to make more sense.

The fact was that I said things I would not have expected to say that night. The fact was that this doggy in my lap was, if not dead, then as good as dead, and I had done nothing physical to change that, that I knew of. The fact was that at one point this dog rose from the dead and started dragging herself around like a crazy dog. The fact was that I thought I heard voices or messages that were coming to me telling me what was going on.

The fact was that I started jumping up and down like a crazed person myself, saying, "I love you, you can do it," thinking I was helping the dog "raise her vibrations." The fact was that this dog walked up to me after all that had happened, on all fours, when her legs had obviously been broken. The fact was that I held my hand over her body and I felt something transferring from my hand to her body.

These were way too many facts that were outside my paradigm for me to feel comfortable in that moment. A moment where I was also very sleepy, tired and very confused as to what was really happening. I figured, that if Ciccina and I had communicated earlier about the vibrations and the love, etc., then quite possibly we were communicating at that point. And if we were communicating, then what she was telling me was she was going to live through the night, which was a good start.

In my heart of hearts I not only wanted her to live but I somehow knew she was not only going to live through the night, she was going to be better in a really short time. How I knew this, again, I do not know. I also knew that it would require some work. I knew it. Marco had told me and now she had told me. What I didn't know was, what kind of work? I trusted that just as the answers seemed to be coming that night, the answers would come the next day and I would know what kind of work, what to do and how to do it, when the time came.

I lifted Ciccina up and carried her close to my body as to not allow her to move, as I walked into the office toward her bedding. But I didn't lay her down on her bedding. Instead I grabbed her bedding and did something I thought I would never do. I took her bedding into my room, and placed her bedding on the floor in front of my bed, so I could keep an eye on her throughout the night. Assuming I would sleep, should I wake up or should she make a sound and possibly need me, I would be right there.

In retrospect, I would have placed her on my bed if I my bed wasn't a high bed and I wasn't worried that she might have been disoriented in the middle of the night and didn't want to chance her moving around and falling off the bed. My how things had changed. My how I had changed. I had often heard a saying..." The things we do for love." If it weren't for love, would any of us change? I wonder! There I was again, learning another lesson from Ciccina.

I did not want her up and about in the morning without my being up to watch her and make sure she was okay. So I asked her, out loud, this time, "Ciccina, promise me you will sleep all night and then get up when I get up, okay?" "Okay," she said, and the feeling I got was as if she was saying, "Really, it is going to be fine. We have work to do but we will do it in the morning. In the meantime, let us both get some shuteye."

Speaking of shuteye, "Could she shut her eyes?" I wondered to myself after having seen them glued open for so long. It was hard to look at her knowing her eyes must have been drying and hurting. But I was sure, hurting eyes due to dryness was the least of the pain she had to have been enduring.

Sure enough, she closed her eyes and seemed to be to be fast asleep in no time. As I watched her body rise and fall with every breath she took in her sleep, I gave gratitude for her life that night.

"Thank you God, Thank you Dog! I love you! Goodnight," I gushed. I continued, whispering as I made my way under the covers, without taking my eyes off of Ciccina, "I'll see you in the morning, and you will be feeling so much better. You're a miracle and I love you!"

20 THERE'S GOT TO BE A MORNING AFTER

The next morning came early and with much anticipation on my part, much like Ciccina's and my very first morning. Only that time, the morning came with a lot of big changes. First, Ciccina and I were no longer strangers to each other. Secondly, Ciccina was not sleeping in the office; she was sleeping in my bedroom. Thirdly, and the biggest difference of all, the first morning I looked around the office to see if she had left any "surprises" on the floor. That morning the surprise would be if Ciccina was actually still alive, and if she were alive, the question was: "In what state of aliveness would she be?"

I found that I woke up in the exact position that I was in when I fell asleep, with my head close to the edge of the bed and my face facing where I laid Ciccina on a pillow only a few hours before. All I had to do was open my eyes and I could see Ciccina. Somehow, in a way, I felt that I had been looking at Ciccina all night, with my eyes closed and watching over her. I felt as if we had never left each other's sight or thought, as if we were connected all night.

I opened my eyes and was so happy to see Ciccina's eyes looking right back at me. We stared at each other for what seemed like hours; only we did more than that. There was so much information that was going back and forth, there was no way I could take it all in, in the usual way, nor could I remember it all. It was all nonverbal communication. Not with our hands and bodies, but our minds or... our sixth senses?

What I do remember is that she "told" me that she was there for me and because of me. I didn't understand either of these messages. Certainly the trauma she had gone through was much more hers than mine. I certainly felt like I helped her on her way to recovery, but I still hadn't gotten over my not putting her on a leash, thus in my mind contributing to the accident. If she meant that she was there for me, in the sense because I needed her or because I needed to learn something, I couldn't understand how that was possible, and why? Being there for someone is one thing, but making such a sacrifice for the sake of someone, to the point of almost certain death, is something entirely different.

My mind left those thoughts and went to the joy I felt over the fact that that she was alive. With tears welling up in my eyes, I do remember saying, out loud, as I cracked a half a smile, "You're alive? Oh honey, thank you, thank you."

I could tell she was in fact alive, but it was different than that first morning, or for that matter, every other morning since that first morning. First of all, something big had happened, something had changed, something that made her different, at least in my eyes, and made me different. In fact, the whole world was different. What had happened the night before was something that was not possible in the old world, in my old world, in my old way of being, and in my old way of thinking.

The other thing that was different was that as I looked at my little Ciccina's face, it was not the same face. She was obviously tired, but her face was not the same. Her face was crooked from the accident. As I was waking up, the memory of every moment of the night and morning before started to flood my mind. Second by second I was remembering all the grueling moments. By the time I had woken up completely, looked at Ciccina, and stepped out of the bed toward her, I had relived, in my mind, some of the most horrific hours of my life.

There was something else different that morning. Though obviously not as big a deal as Ciccina's face being mangled, her tail wasn't wagging. That to me was a big deal. Her tail wagging was her signature, and her whole little butt and body that would wag right along with it. That morning her tail did not even move, and frankly, neither did Ciccina, not one inch.

This too was very definitely different. Under normal circumstances, during the day, when Ciccina was asleep, I could not move a muscle without her waking up and eyeing my every move. If I actually got up, at the very least she would lift her head and usually her tail would start wagging. If I then looked like I was making my way to her or toward something that could potentially be exciting to her, like the kitchen or the door, or another room even, she would be up on all fours and ready for whatever.

That morning, as I got out of bed, not only did Ciccina not look like herself, or act like herself, she did not seem to be ready for anything at all. Sadness began to pour over me. I began to wonder if what had happened the night before was a nightmare that turned into a bigger nightmare and I wondered what scary things I might learn as the sun came up that morning.

Was Ciccina not moving because she was blind and couldn't actually see me? Was Ciccina deaf and couldn't hear me, or deaf and blind? Was Ciccina actually paralyzed and couldn't move? Was she not really able to walk? Did her legs, which were obviously broken the night before, not mend during her raising her vibration? Could they have possibly mended that quickly, anyway? And if not, then how did she walk over to me at the end of her frenetic, whatever that was, the night before? What else could be different that morning?

Before I even made my way to Ciccina, all the things that I had stopped thinking of the night before started to fill my head with negativity and fear. What if she did have internal bleeding? What if her mouth were cut and her teeth were broken? Obviously there were cuts; there was blood on the street and blood on her and on the bedding and me. What if she had crushed bones? What if, what if?

I never even gave her something to ease her pain. I might not have thought of doing that anyway. Years earlier during my own health journey, I had given up all drugs, prescription and over the counter, and I didn't even have any in my place. I didn't even have any natural painkillers or anything like that. I also couldn't have left her to go get some last night, nor could I have taken her with me. And I wouldn't have known which of the painkillers would have been safe for dogs and what dosage. I just wouldn't have known.

"Poor Ciccina," I said in my mind to her, "How is it that you say you are living because of me when I did nothing to help you?" Such a strong sense of guilt came over me.

All those thoughts had happened in a matter of seconds, or a minute or two at the most, as I slowly made my way out of my bed after having retained her gaze for what seemed to be a lifetime and took the two steps toward her and sat down on the floor next to her.

The moment my hand touched her small body, all the voices and questions in my head stopped. There was silence. I had a sense that there was serious work to be done and things were about to change again for Ciccina and for me, and in another big way. Exactly what I was feeling or "knowing," I wasn't sure. But whatever I "knew," it was no joke and it was serious and we were going to have to get started right away.

What I heard was, "I'm not myself this morning, but I'm gonna make it if you help me." Tears flowed from my eyes as I felt there was a pact being made between the two of us, Ciccina, and I, and we were going to do this. I had no idea what I was agreeing to, but it felt big. Whatever it was seemed like a daunting task, an impossibility, but something was saying it was possible... probable... likely... and finally, once I was able to get out of my way again and the questioning stopped, it felt certain!" "Ciccina," I started to speak, with a lump in my throat, "you're gonna be fine, right?" I questioned, at first. "Right Ciccina?" "You're gonna be fine, I know you are. You're a good dog, you're beautiful and you're amazing." "You ARE going to be fine, I just know it."

"I need your help," I distinctly heard or felt Ciccina say with words that vibrated right to the center of my gut. "What can I do?" the words came through audibly, though my tears had turned to a quiet sob.

I think I was sobbing because I was partly confused, and partly in fear, and partly not knowing what was going to happen from that point on. I was having a conversation in my mind, or within my sixth sense, and I was risking Ciccina's life on it, and yet, it sounded like and felt as real, if not more real, if that were possible, than any other conversation I had ever had in my life.

The other thing that spurred on the tears and sobbing, I came to understand, was that; again, I knew that there was something big about to happen, bigger even than a sixth sense conversation. Though I wasn't sure exactly what it was, I knew it was so big that it made me wonder how I was going to handle it.

As if the whole experience of the night before hadn't left me baffled and bewildered, confused and amazed, I knew it wasn't over and there was more to come. From that moment on, much like the night before, it was as if I was in an altered state. At least, it felt to me like I was in an altered state. I don't know how to describe it really; I just wasn't feeling like my normal self.

I wasn't thinking like I normally did either. Of course I wasn't thinking like my normal self, I was talking to a dog, and she was responding to me. Better yet, for the most part, we weren't even talking, we were communicating telepathically, or something like that. And, what we were "communicating" about, weren't the normal things I would be communicating about with a person, much less a dog.

From that moment on, it was just Ciccina and I. We had made a pact, we were on a very important mission, and it was between her and I. And, if I believed what I had heard Ciccina say, it was for me that we were doing this. If even it was remotely for me, I was going to make sure to get the most out of it, and for Ciccina too.

From that moment on, no more thought of involving a veterinarian entered my consciousness. I didn't even share this with my friends who had dogs or with anybody else. I shut myself out from the world, excused myself from some obligations, meetings and such, and allowed for what would/could happen in that "altered space" and time.

What Ciccina needed from me, I wasn't sure, but at that moment I knew what I needed, badly. I needed to relieve myself, since I hadn't done that yet this morning. Recalling the trauma and drama that happened the night before when I left Ciccina's sight for just a moment, I was in a quandary. I wasn't exactly sure what she would or could do if I were out of her sight. At the same time, I had never had an animal in the bathroom with me, and having a dog in the bathroom with me did not feel like a comfortable solution.

That morning was no time for modesty, old "rules," or any rules, for that matter, as I would come to find out. I had a legitimate reason for doing what I knew I needed to do. Besides, we had been through her almost death together; certainly we could make it through that. It was something that was only going to last a few minutes anyway and it would soon be over.

At that point I still wasn't sure if Ciccina could walk or not, and I didn't want to pick her up just yet. I grabbed two corners of the pillow on which she was lying and I pulled her toward the open bathroom door in my bedroom. I then turned the pillow around so she could face me. Argh! Unfortunately, the way my bathroom toilet was situated in the Master Bath, it was directly across from the door, and facing in her direction. There was no where else for her to look, in her immobile state, except right at me as I went about my business.

Moments later, there I sat, eye to eye with Ciccina. She was watching me do what I had seen her do every day, several times a day, for months. Somehow I would rather watch her than have her watch me. But there I was, breaking my last stand out rule, no dog in the bathroom. I felt like there was nothing left. We had broken down all my barriers, walls and rules. After all that, there I was tired, raw, unnerved, confused, heartbroken, sad... and sitting doing my business in front of a dog.

Even still, none of that was terribly important anymore at that moment. What was important, was that after I had taken care of my immediate needs, I needed to figure out what Ciccina's needs were. In all that time, she had not gotten up from the same exact position she was in when I laid her on the pillow the night before. She had not relieved herself either, like she did every morning

I once again sat next to her and started to pet her as I thought to myself, "What are we going to do with you?" Without thinking too much about it, or waiting for an answer from wherever the answers were coming, I gently picked her up and held her close to my body. Together we went to get her leash and I put it on her. Though I knew she wouldn't or couldn't go very far or very fast, I wasn't taking any chances. This was one lesson I was never going to forget.

I wasn't even sure if she would be able to stand on all fours, much less walk. I held her and then, with no fanfare, no "Wanna go bye, bye," no "Wanna go for a walk?" nothing, I unceremoniously walked out the front door with her still in my arms. There was no tail wagging, no happy barking at me or at the door, no scratching at the wall in anticipation of the door opening. Nothing.

Quietly, we made our decent down the same stairs where only hours before she, seemingly possessed, ran down to what I thought for sure was her demise. This time however, she was in my arms and nothing was the same. At the bottom of the stairs, I placed Ciccina down on a small patch of grass that she always smelled but that never served as her "spot," since it was at the bottom of stairs. Either it was too close to home or I figured she was always stringing me along, or "leashing" me along, I should say, prolonging her relieving herself, to prolong her walk. I had gotten that early on, and I understood. There was such a lot of grass out there, why settle for the first grass you see. Sniff a little.

But that day was not a day for sniffing. I wasn't even sure if her nose could sniff and if she could smell. Her nose was so bent out of shape along with the rest of her face that it was hard to even look at her. Her features where so out of place and her head looked squashed. Of course I also knew how she looked before and knew why she looked the way she did. It was just not a pleasant sight nor did I like the thoughts that went with it. But I had to deal with it and I still didn't know quite how.

I placed Ciccina down on the little plot of grass and she just lay there for a moment. When she didn't move at all, all the scary thoughts came back to me, like, "Can she walk? Do her internal organs even work?"

At the same time these thoughts where going on in my head, I was also remembering how it used to be. I thought about all the things she had taught me on our walks, and how she enjoyed them. I wondered if she would ever enjoy them again. I wondered and worried about whether she could not only walk, but smell. Smelling was so important to her, but then again, so was seeing. I still couldn't tell if she could see or not.

Even though, when we "communicated" telepathically, it looked like she was looking right at me. But then again, I thought, if she really was communicating telepathically, then she could probably sense where I was sitting and look towards me. Then there was touching, hearing, tasting, I wondered, had she lost all of these? What would life be without them? How precious these seemingly lesser senses are, until something happens and some of them are gone. What is a dog without its senses? For that matter, what are we without our senses?

For a moment I thought about how I didn't use my senses enough and how she had been teaching me to use them and to truly experience the world with them. How ironic would it be that the being that opened up my senses had lost the capacity to use hers? How sad would it be? "Poor Ciccina," I thought, as tears started to come to my eyes again, while I watched her just lay on the grass, not moving, incapacitated.

As I was crying a different thought came to my mind. I remembered how what I thought, said and felt must have been affecting her. That was straight from the message from the night before, wherein I was helping her "raise her vibrations," and sending her love.

I came to my "senses" and remembered understanding how we/she was powerful beyond my comprehension and that there was something going on beyond the normal in that moment. For all I knew it was something that was always going on, I just was not aware, like living a life without one of my senses. In that case, that sense was a sixth sense. Could it be possible that the sixth sense was even more powerful than the other five, and I had been living without it all along? At least, the awareness of it?

Still that was something that I did not understand. Understand it or not, it was something that I did not want to get in the way of. And, in fact, I wanted to understand it.

Recalling what I was doing the night before with jumping up and down, "raising my vibration," sending Ciccina love, visualizing and saying words of encouragement out loud, I started to think of how I could use these same techniques to support her in that moment.

"You can do it Ciccina," I started to say over and over, as I started changing my thoughts. I took a happier more vibrant tone of voice, and instead of "Poor Ciccina," and the feelings that went with it, I started thinking and saying, "You are strong, Ciccina, you are powerful. You can do it!"

I knelt down beside her on the grass and started to lift her up a bit, all the while saying things like "Come on Ciccina, you can do this, I believe in you. Let's do this together." As I gently lifted her, she carefully started to move her legs down beneath her. I started crying again. I couldn't help it, seeing her struggle as she did was hurting me. At the same time, I was crying because she was doing it. It was as if she could hear me. She had almost instantaneously changed her position when I started with the words of praise.

"Come on Ciccina, there you go, I love it, you're doing it!" I exclaimed out loud through the tears.

In that moment there was nothing, no grass, no stairs, no neighbors, no street, only Ciccina and I. The world had stopped but for Ciccina. I was watching every small movement her body was making to see if she was moving her legs awkwardly, placing her feet on the grass sure-footedly, and whether she would eventually stand on her own. Slowly, painstakingly, but surely, she stood, on her own, but with me keeping my hands at her side gently to not hurt her, but for stability, just in case. "Brava Ciccina, Brava!" I exhaled as if I had been holding my breath throughout the whole arduous process.

At that point, I was ready and hoping for a movement of another kind. Something made me feel that if she could have a bowel or bladder movement, or preferably both, we would have been in better shape than all the horrors I was imagining, at that time. I was kneeling there for minutes watching her intently; ironically, like Ciccina seemed to be staring at me while I was doing the same in the bathroom only minutes before. Sure enough, after a few more minutes Ciccina had a movement.

I was never so happy to see her do her business as in that moment. How interesting that the little things like having a bowel movement can be moments of joy, moments of strong confirmation, moments of upliftment. I thought to myself that I would never take anything, not even a bowel movement for granted again.

I held Ciccina's leash as she finished and slowly turned her crooked face to look at me with her sad pitiful eyes from which I still managed to feel they were saying to me, "I did it." And she had.

She had done "it," but all was still not right in her and my world. After a moment of gratitude and hope, my thoughts turned to "What else can she do?" I knew that whatever she could do, it would have to be taken really slow. I knew that part of my "job" would be to stay in tune with her and let her lead me. Not only did she know what she could do, better than I did, as evidenced by what had happened the night before, I also wanted to make sure I didn't hurt her in any way by pushing her to do anything she couldn't or wasn't ready to do.

I went to pick her up, but to my surprise and elation, she started to take a slow but methodic step. Slowly and carefully, she stepped as if measuring each movement of each leg and foot, or better yet, as if walking for the first time, ever. In essence it was her first time walking on the ground since the accident. Ciccina had come back from the dead and those were her first steps as a dog on earth again. I couldn't have been happier and more proud of her and I wanted to make sure she knew it.

Besides my "Ciccina, you're walking! You can do it, Ciccina" that I repeated over and over, I was trying to concentrate intently, visualizing her walking, to help her along. I don't know how else to describe what I was doing. Again, I was thinking of the night before and how I was jumping up and down trying to "raise my vibrations" for her. In a similar way I thought if I visualized enough, she would feel my thoughts, or see them, or whatever might happen. It didn't make sense to me at the time, but then again, in my old way of rationalizing things, none of that did.

Still I visualized. While thinking as hard as I could, Ciccina took a few steps toward the stairs. Upon getting to the bottom of the stairs, she slowly turned her head to look at me and I knew exactly what she wanted, and needed from me at that moment. I leaned down and gently picked her up, and carried her up the stairs and back inside.

Wait, she looked at me? She turned her head and looked at me. She could see? She could see! I was sure of it. My heart jumped with excitement, but it was just for a moment. As exciting as that was to me, there were so many other things to think about.

Once inside, I got a little bowl out of the cupboard that I had never used for her before and filled it up with some water and held it up to her. She drank, not too much, but she drank. What a relief. That was exciting, even though she only drank a little bit, I was happy with that. I didn't think she was ready for food, or should I say, I didn't "feel" that she was ready for food, so I didn't even attempt to feed her.

I grabbed the bowl and placed it in my room next to her pillow. I gathered a few other things I thought I would need for our next few hours together before placing her down on the pillow and sitting myself down next to her. We were on a mission and we had work to do. We were going to do it, together.

21 WONDER OF WONDER, MIRACLES OF MIRACLES

I needed some help and I really didn't know where to turn. I needed specialized help, someone who would understand what was happening. At that point, even the thought of contacting friends who had dogs or professionals was not even coming to my mind. In a way it's scary to think that my mind may have been failing me and on the other hand I think, maybe I wasn't supposed to think of those traditional ways.

I had every intent of going the route of hospital and veterinarians the night before and did everything I could, in the moment, to get her to a hospital, until the moment changed and became something "out of this world."

But that morning we were back in the three dimensional world, and I needed some help with what to physically do to help Ciccina back to health. Part of me honestly thought that there was no way that this would ever happen, I just couldn't "see" it, my "mind" couldn't go there. It wasn't possible, at least the way I was "thinking." She was squashed in the middle of the street. Her head was still smashed and even with all that I had seen, it still seemed hopeless at that moment.

On the other hand, I believed it was more than possible. Between what I had witnessed the night before and the improvement she had already made there was indeed hope. Besides, I had made a pact with the dog and in essence said that I trusted her, or whomever was sending me messages or talking to me in my head, and that we were going to do it.

The first and only person that came to mind as far as someone who could help Ciccina and I in this particular situation was Dorothy. Interesting that it would be her. I hadn't known Dorothy for very long and the last time I had spoken to her about the dog, she had said something that I hadn't wanted to hear. She was the one who had shared with me how I would have Ciccina until I learned from her, and once I did she would find a home. When I had called her to tell her my family was going to adopt her, she wasn't convinced that it was going to happen and felt I would be going back home with the dog, which I did.

As I was thinking of calling Dorothy, I remembered all her words and wondered, could what had happened have been the lesson? Could I be right in the middle of it right now? What was it? I wanted to get it for Ciccina and for me. It didn't feel good in that moment to think that Ciccina was going through all that pain to teach me a lesson. Though I didn't understand it exactly, if it were the case, I wanted to make sure I learned the lesson, and fast. I had a higher purpose, a reason beyond myself for learning. I had to do it for Ciccina.

I caressed Ciccina, talked to her and I watched the clock. It felt too early in the morning to call Dorothy. Ciccina and I had gotten up very early, in fact, Ciccina and I had not slept much at all and we were again both very sleepy. I could see her eyes close as I caressed her, which felt good and right. First of all, she was closing her eyes, and secondly, I felt like her body needed the rest. I watched her shut her eyes, and I took that as a good sign.

I was feeling like I was going to be shown little glimpses of hope and that we would recover her health, or her rebirth, so to speak, little by little. But I couldn't wait another little bit to discover what it was that I was supposed to do and for some reason I felt that Dorothy had an answer for me. I contemplated calling her and though it was still too early in the morning, I called her anyway.

Thankfully Dorothy answered the phone, and answered it with a "Tell me what's happening," or something like that, as if she knew something was going on. Of course, she might have thought that something must be going on for me to call her that early. But I felt like she knew something was up.

And so began my agitated and tearful recounting of my story, starting from Ciccina and the Fourth of July parties and ending with, what seemed like an hour later, where we were that morning.

"Wow, honey, you healed her!" were the first words out of her mouth, "Congratulations!"

"Healed her?" I thought, and said out loud, "I was the one who didn't put a leash on her. I was the one who didn't lean down to grab her quick enough when she started barking at someone across the street..." I tried to continue blaming myself, but she stopped me by not only speaking out, but also saying the following words.

"They told me something big was going to happen but they didn't tell me it would be this big. They said you would create a miracle, and I knew it would involve Ciccina, but I didn't think it would be bringing her back from the dead."

I cried and protested, "I didn't do anything, if anything, I was the one who caused her to get hurt."

"No honey," she insisted, "you are who they told me you are, and you are here to show the world how it's done!"

"Dorothy," I protested all the louder, "I didn't do anything. She did it all. She is magical."

"You are both magical and you did it together. She couldn't have done it without you," she continued.

I was beginning to regret having called Dorothy. I guess I wanted someone to beat me up for having been such a bad caretaker of that poor little dog and then to tell me what to do. Instead

Dorothy wanted to convince me that this was all "written in the stars" and that I had brought her back to life after her deadly experience. I felt like we were talking about two completely different incidences.

Regardless, whomever had "told" her that something big was going to happen, could it have been that "they" had told her what it was that I was supposed to do, I wondered? "What am I supposed to do now?" I asked her.

"Continue healing her. You have to finish the job honey. You're just getting started. Everything is going to be different from now on, you'll see. Now that you know what you can do..." I interrupted her, "I didn't do anything," I insisted and cried all the more.

Somewhere, in my heart of hearts I knew there was some truth to what Dorothy was telling me, and quite possibly 100% truth. How this little one had come into my life had always been very suspicious to me. How she acted as if she knew me once she was placed in my arms, that first night, felt very familiar, almost familial.

How the animal shelter that I had known of for years near where I lived was suddenly gone. No one claimed her. No one could find her a home. No one "wanted" her. Laura didn't think she was her dog. I had to keep her until I had the time to bring her to my Mother's in case my family "wanted" her, but no. Everyone kept saying that she was my dog. Dorothy was telling me that she would be my dog until I learned what I needed to learn from her and then I would find her the perfect home.

All of this had become more and more suspicious, and then there was what Dorothy was telling me. Dorothy was telling me things that I couldn't believe or didn't want to believe, about me and about Ciccina, and about what had happened. It was far beyond anything that I had thought possible. It sounded "supernatural" and woo woo to me. It was not possible. It was too confusing.

I quietly resigned to agree to disagree without letting her know it, but I wanted to know what she thought I should do to help

Ciccina. "Use your energy," she said, matter-of-factly.

"What energy?" I retorted. I was trying to help this dog back to health here and she was talking to me about "energy?" "The same energy you used last night to bring her back from the dead." Again, she said it, so matter-of-factly, as if she was telling me to open a can of dog food and feed it to her.

"Dorothy, I'm serious, I don't know what to do and I don't know what you're talking about," I pleaded, "Help me!"

"Well Darlin', I'm telling you, but you don't believe me," she started in on me, "You have powers that I've been trying to tell you about. We all have them, but they aren't activated in all of us. 'We' activated your powers the day you and I met. 'They' told me you were going to use them in a big way, but I didn't think you would do so, so soon, and this big. I've never brought a dog back from the dead. Obviously, you're ready for what you've come here to do."

Again I interrupted her. I wasn't in the mood for flattery or confusing talk about my purported powers, or what my mission in life was, for that matter. Not at this moment at least. But since I didn't think she was going to stray from her line of thinking at that moment, I figured I would just go along with it. So I asked her, "Okay Dorothy, then what can I physically do to bring that energy out to heal Ciccina."

"The energy comes out of your hands Darlin', you don't need anything else. But if you want to use a tool, use that Chakra Box I gave you for your Birthday, and use the pendulum to transfer the energy," she said.

"The Chakra Box, I didn't think of that, that's a good idea," I finally agreed with her. The Chakra Box was something that I was very fond of for reasons beyond my understanding. In fact, the Chakra Box was something that felt very familiar to me and something that I wanted and wished I could have from the moment I had laid eyes on it.

The fact that the Chakra Box felt familiar to me never struck me as being odd, even though I had never seen one or heard of one before. When Dorothy visited LA, the first time I met her, she came to visit and stay at my friend Marco's place. She brought many "tools" of her trade with her, healing equipment, crystals, stones, books, pendulums, etc. Among these things was a beautiful wooden box that was closed with a latch, when I first saw it.

Although there were a lot of beautiful and interesting things to see, I immediately gravitated to the box and opened it. I imagine my eyes must have sparkled as I marveled at what was inside. Inside was a stone representing and holding the tuned energy frequency of each of our chakras in our bodies, though I didn't know this at the time. Alongside each of those stones, was a little vial of essential oil which carried the resonance of the corresponding stone and chakra. And completing the contents of the box was a stone pendulum.

No one had ever told me this, I had never seen anything like this nor had I used it or had one used on me. I just felt like I knew that's what it was, and in fact, later learned I was correct, and was thrilled to be beholding it. I played with it a little bit, starting to balance out my own chakras, or so I thought I was doing, and perhaps indeed was, and getting the feel of the instrument before I heard Dorothy coming into the room. Upon hearing Dorothy I quickly put it away thinking I should not have been touching her tools, especially one as precious as this.

The next time Dorothy came to visit she was once again over Marco's house. This time there were several people over at his place. Word had gotten out that Dorothy was a healer of healers and people in LA were looking forward to meeting her during that visit. While she was in another room talking, or working on someone, I eagerly searched the living room to see if she had brought the chakra box. Sure enough, she had, and I opened it up and ogled it again.

My friend Peter happened to be there, and I beckoned him over and asked him if I could "balance his chakras energetically?" He said, "sure, but what does that mean?" "I don't know," I answered. "What do you mean you don't know?" he laughed nervously.

"Don't worry, it's going to be good for you," I quickly responded, giving him no chance to argue. I wanted to use this box and its contents in the worst way and I had to do it before Dorothy was finished with whomever was in the other room and before she walked back into the living room.

To reassure him that he would survive this experience, I took the pendulum out of the box and I held his hand and opened his palm and held the pendulum over it. I then asked out loud to whomever I thought I was talking to, "Is it safe for me to clear Peter's Chakras for the good of all involved," or something like that. The pendulum circled, and circled to the right, which to me indicated, yes, and I said to him, "See? You're going to be fine."

I quickly took out the first stone in the box and had him hold it in his left hand. I then held his hand with my left hand. In my right hand I held the pendulum over his open palm. The pendulum began to spin, then spin more and faster.

"Wow," I said, "you are so out of alignment."

"What do you mean? What is out of alignment?" he queried.

"Your root chakra," I responded with confidence.

"How do you know?" he questioned further.

"Because the pendulum is swinging," I answered as if I knew.

"Well, what does that mean?" he persisted with his curiosity.

"It means you are not grounded or something like that, I really don't know," I answered honestly.

"Well, if you don't know, what are you doing then?" he asked as he laughed at the situation.

"I'm aligning your chakras, that much I know. Just be quiet," I insisted.

He laughed some more, and like the faithful and ever trusting and loving friend that he is, he let me do my "experiment" or better yet, healing/aligning on him. I had never studied the chakras of the body but I had seen pictures and read a little bit about them in passing in certain books that I had read over the years. I had also never had chakra work done on me of any kind. All this was new to me and very exciting, for some reason.

"Don't you feel something?" I asked him, "I do," I affirmed my own question before he had a chance to answer.

"I feel like there are a bunch of pins on my palm," he said as he tried to explain the sensation he was feeling on his palm.

"You mean like it's tingling, right?" which is what I thought he meant.

"Yes, just like that," he agreed.

"Good," I said proudly, "I'm glad."

The pendulum stopped soon after I said that and I removed the stone from his hand and I placed another one in it.

"Why did it stop spinning?" Peter asked me.

"Because, it balanced your chakra as much as your chakra would accept being balanced at this point." I answered, again, with confidence.

"How do you know that?" he continued.

"Because the pendulum stopped," I abruptly answered, "Now let me do this."

Peter laughed again and shook his head and started taking in the experience.

I was so into what I was doing that I did not notice that Dorothy had walked into the room. While I was doing something I thought was really special, I heard Dorothy say, "What do you think you're doing?" I had been caught and I didn't know how she would react. On the one hand, it was no big deal because I didn't break anything and I didn't use anything up. I could simply replace the stones into the box, the pendulum and all, and close it up, and no harm done.

As I saw it, the problem was, that I was using it without asking her permission. Secondly, I was thinking that this tool was tuned to her somehow and I shouldn't have even been touching it with my hands or my energy. Knowing all this, it still didn't keep me from feeling the desire, almost need, and definite attraction to opening the box and "playing" or "working" with it. And because of my childlike curiosity, I had now been caught and would have to suffer the consequences and at least apologize.

"What do you think you're doing?" again Dorothy asked.

I was too afraid she was going to be upset to notice that her tone was more inquisitive than upset, but nevertheless, I responded nervously. "I was just playing with them, I'm sorry. I hope I didn't ruin anything. I know I should have asked you first."

"No, that's okay, I just want to know what you think you are doing?" she said with an emphasis on the word "think."

Getting her meaning, I responded that I was thinking that I was clearing his chakras, "That's what this is for, isn't it?"

"Yes, but, how did you know how to use it?" she continued. "How did you even know to place the stone in his hand and where did you learn how to use a pendulum like that?"

I just looked at her not knowing what to say. I was also a little bit embarrassed because everyone in the room was now looking at us and in my mind I was still being scolded. Scolding me was far from her mind, quite the contrary actually, as I got from her next comment.

"I've just never seen anyone pick that up before, much less use it like they knew what they were doing."

Peter broke the tension in the moment and announced that he had to leave. He laughed as he thanked me for the chakra clearing, undoubtedly recalling the humor of the previous moment, and left.

A few other people had to leave and we thankfully were distracted enough from my embarrassing situation that we all forgot about the chakra box thing and went on to something else, or at least, so I thought. A little later, Dorothy's daughter Tricia came over to me and explained what the chakra box was. Evidently there was more to the box that I didn't know. It had elements and symbols embedded behind the stones. It was also made of several different handcrafted wood pieces from different parts of the world, and so on and so forth. She explained all this to me and then proceeded to tell me how many hundreds of dollars it had cost her and that she had given it to her Mother as a gift years ago.

I thanked Tricia for the information but in a way was feeling like she was telling me all this to say, "And that's why you shouldn't have been playing with it." In retrospect, it wasn't how she meant it either. I got to know Tricia better as time passed and she didn't seem like that kind of person who would say something in that way and mean something else. It was just me yet again expecting a reprimand and interpreting it as such, when it wasn't.

At the end of the evening, I looked for Dorothy to say goodbye to her and found her wrapping something up in a purple velvet cloth. When I told her that I wanted to say goodbye and thank her, she turned to me, lovingly looked at me, and handed me the item she had just wrapped.

It was heavy and sturdy and felt a lot like the Chakra Box I had played with a couple hours earlier. "What is this?" I asked.

"Unwrap it," Dorothy answered.

"Well what's it for?" I wanted to know before unwrapping it.

"It's your Birthday present," she answered.

"My Birthday is not for a couple months," I answered.

"Just unwrap it," she said as she sighed heavily, as if to say, "Why are you being so difficult?"

Sure enough it was the Chakra Box. "What's this for?" I asked surprisingly.

"I told you, it's for your Birthday." she repeated.

"But I don't understand," I answered. This would be the first time I said, "I don't understand," to Dorothy, but it wasn't to be the last.

She went on to tell me, how she had had the Chakra Box for years and that no one had ever opened it. In all her classes and workshops, and with many clients that have come and gone, no one ever opened it. "No one had ever known what to do with it, until now," she said.

"'They' told me to bring it, and I couldn't imagine why because I hardly ever used it myself, and didn't think I would need it at Marco's. But they told me there would be someone here who would know what to do with it. And it's you," she said happily.

"Take it, it's yours, it's not mine anymore, it's yours." she repeated as she saw me start to hand it back to her.

"Enjoy it honey and put it to good use," she softly said to me as she hugged me goodbye.

"Put it to good use?" Did "they" know, whoever "they" are, that only a few months later, Dorothy would tell me to use it to heal a dog?

22 WE'VE GOT MAGIC TO DO

As soon as I got off the phone with Dorothy I slowly and quietly got up because I had noticed that Ciccina had fallen asleep and I didn't want to wake her. I also didn't want her to notice that I was going out of the room, even for a second. I got the Chakra Box, which was prominently and proudly displayed on top of the entertainment center in my living room. I returned to Ciccina and sat right next to her again. I opened up the Chakra Box, carefully and knowingly, as if I were a doctor opening a doctor's bag with the tools and remedies he needed inside.

I remember not being able to hold back a smile as I opened it knowing that there was truth to what Dorothy was saying and that there was also great mystery and excitement in the air. I felt as though we were going to be doing some magic.

As a little child I used to enjoy watching two particular TV shows that were popular at the time, "I Dream of Jeannie," and "Bewitched." I watched them religiously and used to practically study them. As I watched, I was mesmerized at the magic that I was witnessing. Of course I knew that on the shows, the magic was all being done by film tricks and it was all "TV magic," but on some level, I truly believed that some of what they did was possible for me to do.

Since I never could learn to wiggle my nose like Samantha on "Bewitched," and since I didn't want to do the Tabatha, child version of the nose thing, I took to crossing my arms and blinking like Jeannie in "I Dream of Jeannie." I would on occasion do this as my way of letting my family know that I was about to do magic. Not that magic ever happened, that I recall, after crossing my arms and blinking, but nonetheless, I did it anyway, quite a bit, as a child.

But on that day, I felt like real magic was about to happen. There was no crossing of my arms and no blinking. I was in a real serious mood. Whether or not there was truth to what "they" told Dorothy, whoever "they" were, of what I was going to do, or whether or not I could do "miracles," as Dorothy suggested, I knew for sure that a miracle was exactly what we needed. Technically, we needed another miracle, since we had certainly had one the night before. The miracle of the day required my utmost attention. We had magic to do, and off to work I went.

I got to working on Ciccina much like I worked on Peter, only not exactly. Obviously, Ciccina couldn't hold the stones in her paws. It was interesting, that as much as I protested to not believe in all that, I was very much enjoying what I thought was happening, and what I felt like while I was doing it. Though Ciccina could not hold the stones, I somehow felt that I could do it for her and that would do the trick. As I extrapolated that thought, I went so far as to think that I could do the exact same thing without even holding the stones. In fact, I thought, I didn't even need the pendulum or the Chakra Box itself, for that matter. I just needed to use my "energy." But I had the tool, the Chakra Box, I liked it, and I wanted to use it.

On the one hand I was, having a hard time believing what Dorothy had told me, and yet I was working all that out in my head and convincing myself. Admittedly, it was confusing, but I didn't stop to dwell on it too much longer. We had magic to do. As far as I was concerned, what I had seen the night before proved to me that magic and miracles were possible. In my opinion, the "coming back to life" part was the hard part. After all, it was a spontaneous healing of sorts. I started to call it, "raising the vibrations and self healing." No matter what I called it, it still seemed unbelievable, and even more so for a dog.

According to the pendulum, Ciccina's body was spent, and the pendulum spun for what seemed like hours on each of her chakras. I added a twist for Ciccina however that I had not done on Peter. All the while that I was holding the stone with the back of my left hand with the stone in it touching her, I was repeating a mantra of sorts, in my head, for her.

"You are healed, Ciccina, you are healed. You are love Ciccina, you are love. I am proud of you Ciccina, I am proud of you. You can heal yourself Ciccina, you can heal yourself. You are amazing Ciccina, you are amazing." I kept repeating phrases like that over and over again in my head while the pendulum spun and the stone in my hand touched her delicate little body.

I painstakingly took as much time as the pendulum needed; and as Ciccina lay there, I felt, her taking it all in. All the time I took with her was time I was taking away from getting ready to go on a trip, a little more than a week from that day. I still did not have my luggage packed or for that matter my show and my music all prepared for almost a week's worth of performances and appearances, etc. I also had to get caught up on everything that I was doing because I couldn't leave so many things undone in my business, for a week.

I had to work, and yet my most important work in that moment felt like it was taking care of Ciccina and nursing her back to optimum health. Of course, my performances were important as was my work and somehow I had to do it all. Wherein I would under normal circumstances already have been stressing out about all that needed to get done, I had added healing a dog from a fatal, or near fatal car crash to the mix, and I was calmer than ever.

As the day went by I remained reclusive. Except for the business phone calls I was scheduled to make, and the occasional call to Dorothy and my Mother, I didn't call anyone or even answer the phone. I worked on Ciccina and I worked on my business, and I worked on my performances and that's all. Even the calls to my Mother were shorter than normal and I never shared with her what had happened or what was happening. I think I was thinking that I didn't want anyone to tell me that it couldn't be done. I think I didn't want anyone else to feel sad or sorry for Ciccina. Somehow I was thinking that this wouldn't ultimately help Ciccina. I don't know why I thought that, but I did.

Ciccina and I had an understanding. We were communicating constantly. We had developed a schedule and a plan that we devised together. I was to watch and listen and let her guide me. I was convinced that this was all real. That Ciccina and I were really communicating. That we really were going to co-create another miracle. That there would be more raising of vibrations and spontaneous healing. And that my job was to support whatever it was that was doing the magic, and most of all, to stay out of the way.

Day One I just stayed with her all day. She didn't eat that day, but that didn't worry me, in fact, I understood. I figured her body was busy rebuilding and needed lots of rest, sleep and love. I did keep putting water up for her though, throughout the day, and slowly, painstakingly, but surely she would drink, some. Then back down her head would go. I took her outside a second time later in the day, again, I kept her in my arms until I placed her on the same patch of grass. She did do her business and then that time, didn't even attempt to walk. Ciccina just looked up at me and I knew exactly what she was saying. I picked her up, brought her up the stairs, and back into my bedroom we went.

The majority of the day was spent with my Chakra Box at hand, and my "clearing" her Chakras and then waving my hand over her, back and forth, giving her energy and love. Though I can't say that I knew what I was doing for certain, at the time, I was doing it anyway, believing something was happening. I trusted Dorothy's knowing, though I wasn't sure about everything else she told me. And also, the more I did it, the more things would come to my mind, things I had heard or read that had to do with energy, energy transfer, and healing. My mind which had been "in the way," before, also began to open up to the possibilities that were before us and bring forth from my memory banks, ideas that could work.

I actually didn't stop there, I took out all the stops and tried to appeal to all her senses that she loved to use so much and that she taught me how to use. I placed other pretty crystals that I had, around her, with beautiful colors. It was nothing I would have ever done before because I wouldn't have wanted her playing with them. But I knew that if she opened her eyes, she could see them and it would give her something pretty to look at. Besides, I had heard that the crystals had healing properties and I wanted them near her, just in case that was true.

I played for her ears, my friend Marco's music from his Pets Love Music Series, the "Dog Dreams" CD specifically for Dogs, just like he had told me I should, that night on the phone. Then I sprayed Lavender Oil Aromatherapy that was supposed to have a very calming effect and help induce sleep. I also, while my hand was hovering over her, at times, would lay my hand on her so she could feel my touch. When I was working on other things, I tried to do them near her, and with one hand so I could I could keep my hand on her all day letting her know I was there and giving her energy.

And for her sixth sense, I talked to her all day, not just out loud, but most especially in my head. I told her that she was well and that she was strong. I told her that she was running and jumping. Even more than that, I visualized her that way. I saw us playing again and her jumping on me and licking me. Even though I never let her lick me before, I thought that if she were able to see the picture in her mind, it would be an incentive for her to get better. That was, assuming dogs really did see images in people's heads.

I wasn't sure of where I had gotten all the ideas to do all of this, but I was sure it was good to do them and that they would work. It seemed that, not only was I feeling like I was receiving information or guidance, but I also had my own ideas. Experiences that I had gained over the years, like aromatherapy, etc., was coming to me and feeling useful. The way I had come upon acquiring certain things that then became useful was also interesting.

I started looking into essential oils because I liked cologne but found out I was allergic to it. I came to learn that my body was reacting to the chemicals in modern day colognes and I stopped using them all together. I gave away a lot of designer, brand name colognes and opted instead for essential oils, long before colognes made of natural oils made their way into the mass market. The crystals were something that I always found beautiful and had wanted to have them around. I was also gifted a few from Dorothy, who also insisted I should have them. I wasn't sure why she thought I should have them, but I had started collecting ones I thought were beautiful long before I learned they also had helpful properties, and was only too happy to accept.

As a singer, and musician, I too had started researching the science of music, notes, keys, vibrations, frequencies, etc., and their effect on our body, mind, environment, etc. No coincidence that I met Marco, who was creating music with all that in mind. Again, none of these things could have been coincidences. And at the time they all seemed to be there, ready for me to use for Ciccina's healing.

As the memories came to me of things I had learned, studied, read, heard, and as I made connections with what worked with what and how to do this or that, I was feeling grateful for everything that I was remembering and relearning and had accumulated over the years. I felt as if I was learning some things for first the time. Kinda like when we learn things in school but we never apply them, we forget them. But when we actually get to use the particular knowledge in a practical way in our life, we really learn. I was feeling like I was really getting it. As much empathy and compassion as I was feeling for Ciccina, I was also feeling grateful to her because I was learning and sensing, remembering and feeling so many things that seemed so important all of a sudden.

These things and feelings and knowings seemed so important, and such a part of me, that I wondered how it was that I was living without them before. It was interesting to me that I was learning to "live" because of having been faced with "death." Thankfully not my own death, but the death of a companion, whom I had grown to love and respect, and from whom I had already learned so much. What if in some way, this all was really for me? What if somehow there really was a plan and this was part of a plan? After all, Dorothy had said that I would have to learn a lesson before I found the dog a home. I couldn't imagine a bigger lesson than what I was going through in those days.

Potentially buying in to the possibility that somehow, "cosmically," Ciccina had been part of a plan to help me find answers to questions I had been asking, started to make me feel guilty. And though guilt may have been an appropriate emotion for me to feel, I knew that, if this were the case, then it would defeat the purpose. I also knew that I had to keep my vibrations raised and not think negative thoughts for Ciccina to get better. Instead of guilt I decided that I had to get the lesson, any lesson, because not getting it, after all Ciccina had been through, was not an option!

So I listened, I prayed, I worked and I did everything I could think of, or that came to me in a message form.

When it came time to sleep, or at least for me to sleep, since Ciccina had been sort of sleeping all day, I told her I was going to bed. But more importantly, I told her how proud I was of her. I reminded her that even though she was hurting, she had lifted her head and had taken a drink when I gave her water. And even though she was hurting, she let me take her outside to do her business.

I told her that doing that took a very strong and determined dog and that I was proud of her. I told her that I knew she was working hard on healing herself on many levels and I thanked her for showing me what was possible and teaching me about life and death and living and not dying.

Then I had an idea that we needed to set a goal for her. So I said to her that I wanted to set a goal for the next morning. I told her the goal was that when we got up in the morning, and I took her down the stairs and placed her on the patch of grass, that I didn't want her to do her business there, but to walk at least a few steps and show me she could do it. I told her, that was all she had to do the next day, and I would know she was on her way to recovery for sure.

Of course I let Ciccina sleep in my room, and again, I faced her from my bed and we locked eyes as I laid my head on my pillow. Again, we told each other that we loved each other and I fell asleep.

In the morning, I woke up to a Ciccina whose eyes were still staring at me, but whose head was actually up. I smiled at her and made happy noises.

Her tail did not wag and her body did not move. Her face was still crooked and her eyes were still sad. But I knew this was a new day, and I knew for certain that though it might take time, Ciccina was going to be 100%, if not somehow better than 100%. Though I didn't actually have much time, since I was going to be out of town for a week in a little over a week, I was uncharacteristically calm.

Of course I didn't want to leave Ciccina with anyone in this condition. I wanted to be the one to nurse her back to health. After all, supposedly, this was my job, and my learning. But I didn't worry about it, in fact, I almost didn't even think about it. I just knew everything was going to be okay. On some level I was thinking, if all of this were truly part of a Divine or a Cosmic Plan, then surely the timing of my trip had to have been calculated into that plan.

To look at Ciccina, though, I don't know how I stayed calm, because she was still a mess. Funny though, she was a mess that I loved and she was my mess, and I was going to help her clean up.

After getting up, I looked at her and reminded her of our goal for the day. I told her that I was sure that she could do it and that I was already proud of her even for considering it. I told her that if she achieved the day's goal, that I would be the happiest man in the world, and that she would be most certainly, without a doubt, well on her way to full recovery.

I wasn't sure what full recovery looked like, to be honest. Between not knowing if she would ever walk right and not knowing what might have happened to her brain in all this, it was all to my "scientific" part of the brain, very uncertain. Add to this the fact that I didn't know if what had happened to her face was structural or not, it would, to the casual observer, seem at best very uncertain. I didn't dare touch her face, I couldn't imagine it would feel good to have been touched. I only gently wiped the blood off of it as best I could, and left the rest alone.

Somehow I believed I would touch that face again and better yet, see it back to normal. Something kept telling me to just believe. So, believe I did.

I walked Ciccina outside and down the stairs in my arms. Not only did I not want to push it, I wanted her to be able to have all the strength she could have to achieve "our" specific goal. I wanted her to be able to prove to herself that she could do it, today. I put Ciccina down on the patch of grass in front of the steps. She stood on her own for a second or two and then she looked up at me as if to say, "I'm doing this for you."

The next thing I know, she was walking, slowly, tentatively, determinately, but she was walking. I started cheering her on. "Brava Ciccina, I knew you could do it, and you did it. I love you, you are the best, thank you. Congratulations Ciccina, oh, you did it."

She not only took a few steps, she continued until she had walked half a block. It was in no way like any other time she had walked. She was walking almost sideways, because her body was still crooked, though much less than immediately after the accident. She also was not sniffing. She showed no interest in looking at anything. It was as if she were in a trance. She was concentrating, and all her attention and energy was on the act of walking.

I had been used to walking the whole block with her, not once, but sometimes up to four times, and still sometimes she acted like she wanted more. Most of the time, every time we would get to my steps, she would walk past them, ignoring them. But when she was done, the next time we came around she would walk up them. If I started to walk up the steps after she had walked past them, there would be such a pull on the leash. I would laugh. Sometimes I would do it on purpose just to see where her head was. Sometimes she wouldn't want to turn the corner of the block but go further on to another block, and another, stopping and sniffing all the way. More often than not, she would get her way.

On this particular walk however, at half a block she stopped, and actually did her business, just like in the visualization. I was so proud of her I almost couldn't believe it. After picking up after her I turned to her and crouched down to pick her up, expecting that she would be done walking for the day. Instead she had started to turn herself around and was heading back to the steps.

We slowly made it back to the steps, where I quickly picked her up. I didn't want her to even attempt them, even if she was going to try. She had done so much more than the goal. Back inside, I gently petted her and told her how proud I was again and tried to reward her or entice her with food, but that wasn't meant to be. She did drink however when I brought her back in, more than she had drunk the whole day before, so again, I saw improvement.

Back to the bedroom we went. This time we got what was now her pillow, and we took it into the office. This was the first time she had been in the office since that Fourth of July night I placed her on a pillow for dead. It didn't seem to faze her though. I placed the pillow in a different spot than that night, so as not to bring back any memories for her or me, but in a spot where she could see me at all times, if she chose to.

After a long Chakra clearing session and some energy work and petting, I sat at my desk to work for the first time in all this time. I would glance at her every once in awhile, but she didn't notice. Usually, if she wasn't on my lap, she was sitting somewhere where she could see me. In between her naps she would look up at me and wag her tail, but that wasn't the case that day. She ended up sleeping most of the day in between me giving her water, energy work, and petting.

By evening time, I got much work done and was quite satisfied with what I had done and was ready for bed. I hadn't eaten much myself that day, besides being a little upset with the situation and my not wanting to leave her or cart her around, it was just as well. I was also satisfied with the "work" that Ciccina had done. I didn't know exactly what she had done, but I knew she was working on herself and something inside me felt I needed to accept and be satisfied, so accept I did, and satisfied I was.

As I picked Ciccina and her pillow up to bring them into the bedroom I started telling her what an exciting day tomorrow was going to be. I told her that I saw her walking to the end of the block and back and that afterwards I saw her eating. "Yes," I said out loud, "I see you eating. Not very much, but I want to see you put something in your tummy, okay?"

I was planning on giving her some of the most nutritious food that I had at the time and slipping some powdered green vitamins and minerals into her food to help her rebuild herself.

We said good night much like we had done the nights before. I was getting used to having her in my room, in fact, I was liking it. I didn't sleep on the edge this time, I actually was able to feel comfortable enough with knowing she was going to be okay to turn to face the other direction and sleep in my normal preferred position.

When morning came, there she was again ready to greet me with that crooked smile I had come to expect since the "accident." I hated it and I loved it at the same time. I hated that she looked the way she did, but I loved that she was there and alive and her looks didn't matter to me, as long as she wasn't in any pain. And if she was in pain, we were taking care of that.

That morning I changed the routine a little. That morning I gave her her "energy bath," so to speak, before we went out. I wanted to make sure she had enough energy to take her to the end of the block and that she worked up an appetite. I told her what we were planning on doing and that it was all she needed to do that day. The plan was for us to walk a little farther and then to eat something. Even if it was just one bite, I wanted to see her eat.

I felt a little like my Italian Mother when she would want me to eat. It worked so well, that getting me to stop eating became more like the problem then getting me started. I don't know if it was my Italian upbringing that made me think eating was important for her that day or if the guidance was coming from above, or for that matter, from Ciccina below.

Ciccina was very much below me since she was just a little thing, but in those days, I felt like she stood so far above me. I couldn't imagine having gone through what she had gone through in those past few days. I thought to myself, if something or someone told me to crawl, hop, walk, or run after an injury, and told me that I could raise my vibrations and heal myself, or something like that, I don't know that I could have. Would I have the spirit that this little dog has? Was this another lesson? The courage, strength and love this dog had was incredible and she was doing it all without any medication or sedatives.

Down the stairs I walked with Ciccina in my arms, only this time, I didn't place her on the small patch of grass, I placed her on the sidewalk fully expecting her to walk. I knew in my heart of hearts that she was going to do just like we had decided she would do, the night before. I reminded her just before we left, I visualized it, and we were going to do it, right then.

With a look up at me as if to say, "Here we go," Ciccina started walking. Still slowly, still not caring about her surroundings, still crooked, but she walked. Without stopping Ciccina walked to the end of the block. For a moment I thought she was going to round the corner, but instead, as if on cue as per my visualization, she turned herself around and slowly started back home. Along the way she stopped to do her business a couple times. Unlike how she liked to do, sniffing about, "picking the best spot," this time it was just when she was ready. She stopped, and she went, and then again. Then she walked me back to the steps.

The block which normally took all of a minute to walk must have taken about a half hour, literally. I was in no way going to hurry her along. I did however cheer her on like before and encouraged her every step. Instead of being sad or worried it had taken so long, I was happy that she had done it. She was doing everything just like we had talked about, and I couldn't be happier.

I picked her up at the stairs and when we made it back in, I placed her down on the kitchen floor, a place she was never allowed in before, so she could watch me. I prepared for her what was essentially her first meal. I was so happy to be feeding her, her first meal, and I felt like she was going to honor me by eating. I of course was taking so much of this personally, but truly, it must have been her dictating every step. For all I knew, she was telling me what I was supposed to be thinking and telling her.

I wasn't sure how that all worked. All I knew was that it was working and I was amazed and excited about it.

I picked a can of the moistest dog food that I had. It was the kind that was always her favorite and it was a sure bet that she would eat it, under normal conditions. I put some of my favorite powdered vitamins and minerals in it and I mixed it up real nice, and I placed it right there on the kitchen floor right in front of her. Ciccina eating in the kitchen would have been something that would not have happened a couple days earlier. But that day my little Princess was having her "first meal," or at least a bite or two of it, and I would have been happy spoon feeding her, if that's what it took for her to eat.

And so, this was the case. She looked and looked at it. In fact, I even thought I saw her sniff it, although not for long. I was hoping her sense of smell was intact, but I was hoping she wouldn't be able to detect the greens, because I wanted her so much to have the vitamins and minerals. Regardless, she didn't eat at all, not even one bite.

I reminded her of our goal and that she had fulfilled half of our goal by walking the whole length of one side of the block and back and now she had one more thing to do. I picked up a spoon and I placed it up to her mouth. Her little crooked mouth opened a little and that little tongue of hers came out and started licking around the spoon.

Licking was good, "I'll take that," I thought to myself. She licked and licked until she pried a piece of meat off the spoon and started to chew. "Chew Ciccina, chew, you're doing it, you're eating. Oh, I love you so much, thank you for doing this for me. You're doing it, you are on your way, baby." I exclaimed. I was so proud of her.

I beamed with delight as I knew we were more than on our way.

I spoon fed her each bite until she turned her head away from the spoon and I knew she was satisfied, and so was I. I couldn't have been happier. To me, this meant that we were doing everything right and everything was moving along just fine. Moreover, it meant that whatever we were doing telepathically or subconsciously was working too, and/or that the messages were spot on.

I happily went to work at my desk with Ciccina on the pillow close by, surrounded by pretty crystals with the scent of Lavender in the room, and music from Marco's CD wafting in the air. I caught her looking at me every once in a while, but without the wagging of the tail and the shaking of her body, it just wasn't the same. But I happily accepted it as a welcome improvement.

I so missed her wagging tail. I wanted to see her wag her tail, so badly. Was this too much to ask? Was this too soon? Everything inside me said, it was time for Ciccina to wag her tail. It wasn't for that day, she had already done her part, achieved her goals and done them well. In fact, Ciccina ate later on in the day, again. I still had to spoon feed her, and I was still happy to do it.

Once I got that notion in my head about her tail wagging the next day, I couldn't wait for tomorrow to come, because tomorrow I was going to get to see Ciccina wag her tail. Though I am normally a go to bed late type of person, I couldn't wait to get to bed. I was like a child who went to bed early on Christmas Eve in the hopes that Santa Claus would bring gifts in the middle of the night. And in so many ways, that was the case. Every morning seemed to bring new gifts. As far as I was concerned those gifts were better than Santa Claus', better than Christmas, in fact, they were among the best gifts I had ever received. I had participated in the miracle of life; not birth, life. What material gifts could be better than that?

That night I made Ciccina fully aware of our big plans for the next day. She seemed in full agreement. It made me question, if she agreed, then why didn't she just wag her tail right there and then as she had always done before? Could she still not wag it? Or, "patience and knowing, maybe that is what she's trying to teach me now," I chuckled at the thought. "That's what you are trying to teach me now, aren't you, Ciccina, patience, and knowing, right, patience and knowing.... You're so cute!" I said as I rubbed her, still gently but with more pressure than I had used up till then, since the "accident."

Like it had been proven to me over and over again in the past few days, everything that I was envisioning was happening, but it was happening in progression and everything and both of us were in agreement. I had this knowing that it would happen, I wasn't wondering anymore if it would happen, it was only a matter of time, of that I was sure. But of course, I wanted it to happen right then. I wanted it all right away.

How ironic, had I had it all right away, I would have had nothing compared to what I ended up receiving. I would not have learned anything that I had learned. I would not have grown in the ways that I did.

Had the owner been somewhere near the dog, looking for her when I wanted the owner there that night, "right away," I wouldn't have had to take her home. Had the owner claimed her like I would have wanted her to, "right away," I would not have had those months together with Ciccina. Had Laura taken Ciccina when I wished she had taken her, "right away," I wouldn't have had the learning of the senses. Had my family taken her like I hoped they would have taken her, "right away," I wouldn't have participated in the miracle that was happening in that moment.

As much as I wasn't liking things not happening "right away," I could go on and on as proof to myself that "right away" was not always in my best interest.

During our energy healing session that night, I kept reminding Ciccina that the next day she would wag her tail. "Right Ciccina, you're going to wag your tail tomorrow, aren't you?" I would say over and over. "It's going to feel so good to wag your tail again and I am going to be so proud of you," I encouraged.

We went to bed together again, me in mine, she in hers, in my room, as if we had been doing that all along. Nothing seemed weird or different. Nothing seemed as if it were out of place or wrong. Nothing was ruffled, nothing was bad, everything was perfect as if it was supposed to be that way, just the way it was. Here I was a man and his dog, sleeping in the same room. I still had a clean white down comforter and I still had a clean made up bed. From that new vantage point, I couldn't see what the problem had been before.

In fact, I reflected for a moment, on how it seemed that that little doggy got everything it ever wanted out of me. There was nothing left for me to get or for me to give. She had gotten me to break all my rules, through love. She had gotten me to see things from her perspective, through her eyes. She had gotten me out of my cocoon. She had won, and yet, there she sat, looking at me with those pitiful, beautiful eyes on a journey that was unbelievably hard and undoubtedly painful with not an end in sight.

If that were truly all part of some master plan, then she was truly committed to my growth. But if it had been any other way, it wouldn't have achieved the same results. I got that, and felt selfish in the getting that. Had I been asked, I wouldn't have wanted Ciccina or anybody or anything to have to go through what Ciccina had gone through and was still going through. I wouldn't have allowed it. But I didn't have a choice. And if that was the only way I would learn the lessons and get the answers to my questions, then I affirmed again that night that I would learn. Furthermore, I made a request of God that for my still outstanding questions and my future questions, I wanted to learn them from that point on without pain or injury, whether mine or anyone else's. I was choosing to learn through love and joy, with laughter and fun. No more pain, no more sorrow, no more fear, no more anger, no more suffering. No more! I fell asleep with those affirmations for myself.

When morning came I found myself lying there facing Ciccina, even though I had gone to sleep facing the other direction. When I opened my eyes, my eyes met Ciccina's but then went directly to her bottom. Without being wide awake yet, and remembering why, I automatically went to see if her tail was wagging. I looked and waited and recounted our goal from the night before in my mind over and over again. I went back and forth from looking at her eyes and back at her bottom, and back again, but, nothing.

I started to get a bit disappointed and then thought that I should give her a break. She had done so much and had been through so much at that point that just because "I" wanted her to wag her tail, didn't mean that she was ready to, or that it was the right thing for her. Was I being selfish? Was I pushing her too fast? Would she ever be able to wag her tail again?

I abruptly stopped those negative and uncertain thoughts and reminded myself, that all that was decided was not coming from me and that I should let my ego or my pity for her go, and bring my consciousness back to the learnings we had had together. So far, every goal we had set for her each day prior had been agreed upon by both of us.

And even upon establishing that understanding, without realizing it, disappointment crept in again. I stopped my thoughts again and said to myself, "We had agreed on her wagging her tail today, so disappointment or pity is not serving her or our plan. Remember. Believe. Know that she will wag her tail and do what needs to be done, so it will be so."

"Hi Ciccina, good morning?" I then said to her, with honest cheer and sincerity. After all, I was genuinely happy to see her, as I was every morning, and though I was expecting a wagging tail, it was no need to stop showing her the love and caring that I felt and that she deserved, tail wagging or not. Besides, if the wagging of the tail was "in the cards," then it was going to happen. I thought, "The idea wouldn't have come to me if it wasn't right?" My stopping to reflect on it not happening only served to delay everything. I needed to stay true to the cause and my knowing.

Admittedly, that very thing was new to me. Before all that, I wasn't sure I even had a knowing or that I could be sure of my knowing. All of a sudden, I was sure. I knew, and I knew I knew!

"Ciao Bella," as I had started saying to her on occasion, which is what the Italians say to a pretty girl or a beautiful woman, meaning just that, "hello beautiful girl/woman." Actually, it is also a term of endearment used by friends to female loved ones.

"How are you this morning, huh? How are you this morning? Are you feeling up to a good walk today? You want to go bye, bye, huh?"

Huh? All of a sudden, to my surprise, joy and delight and vocal elation, Ciccina started wagging her tail. Not a little wag, not a short wag, but a full fledged way, as if nothing had ever happened, wag. It wagged as if to say, "I'm here, and I'm back and I'm here to stay!"

She wagged, she wagged! Her tail wagged. We did it, we did it! She fulfilled her goal for the day and it was only three minutes into the day. What a great day that was going to be. I jumped up, though she didn't, but that was okay, one step at a time. I went to her and started to rustle her up as I used to do, almost forgetting to be gentle.

She cringed a little as if to say, "Not so rough Daddy, did you forget, I've been through a lot here?"

"I'm sorry Ciccina, but I'm just so happy," I gushed, as I continued to rustle her up, only much more gently. It was not as fun, but it was what the moment called for.

"Let's go for a walk," I exclaimed.

As excited as I was, I forgot all about picking Ciccina up to go down the stairs. My mind jumped ahead to the way it was as if nothing had ever happened, except I was excited that it was the way it was again. Only when we got to the stairs, was I reminded that it wasn't the way it used to be yet. (I could of course easily have been reminded by looking at her crooked face).

At the stairs, I noticed her stop at the top of them and looking down. I was awakened out of my reverie and reminded that I should pick her up. Only, when I bent down to get her, she had hopped on her own down one step. Shocked, I paused to see what she would do.

To my surprise, she took it upon herself, after pausing, to hop again down another step. I kept a close watch in case she would turn to look at me and ask me to pick her up to go the next seven or eight steps, but no, she paused and hopped herself all the way down.

Since this was far and beyond our goal for the day, I wasn't doing the normal cheering that I did when she was doing what we had talked about her doing. Instead, I was actually holding my breath. I wasn't expecting her to do this at all, we hadn't decided on it the night before, and I was shocked, surprised and of course, overjoyed. Even overjoyed, I kept feeling her determination as she paused and looked at the next step and wondered just how much pain she might be enduring. Walking was one thing, but a hop down a step was another. Still, I was sensing she didn't want my help, and that she was going to do it, and she did, all by herself.

Once again, I had forgotten that my thoughts had power and that she could sense them. Those thoughts weren't helping her, on the contrary they could have been hurting her, hindering her, or at the very least, not supporting her. I had also forgotten that my words had power and had I been shouting out words of encouragement she could have felt stronger as she did that task. Instead she had to do that one on her own, which went to show me that she was doing it all herself, and maybe the only reason she needed me at all was for me to learn from her, to be more like her.

That was a humbling thought and experience, my learning that from a dog who had been through so much and was still in the process of recovering. What was also difficult for me, was that she didn't even look up at me once during her process down the steps. It was all her. She was focused on her task and since I wasn't helping, or worse, potentially making matters worse with my thoughts, she wanted no part of it, and did it on her own.

At the bottom of the step, with one last hop, Ciccina started her walk like nobody's business. She walked with her head held higher than the days before. Ciccina seemed to be more interested in what was going on around her as she walked, than the day before. She even started to audibly sniff.

Like during many walks before, I was living vicariously through Ciccina's walk that day, only that day was extra special. That day, Ciccina's attitude seemed to say, "I'm here world, and I'm great. How are you?" "Good to see you! And it's good to be seen!"

Ciccina paraded down the block all the way to the corner. This time instead of turning back, she turned the corner, in more ways than one. We were venturing out. I talked to her and told her how proud I was of her, but she didn't seem to pay me any attention. For a moment my ego wondered if she was ignoring me because I had abandoned her on the steps, as far as not being sure she could do it, and not cheering her on.

Then I got out of that guilty mindset and tried to connect more with Ciccina to see if I could tell what she really was thinking. "I'm happy to be out and about. I'm happy I turned the corner. I've missed everyone and everything. I'm happy to be alive," is what I got from her.

At that point my eyes welled up with tears again for a few reasons. I wondered how many times had I assumed things from my ego self centered, fearful, hurt place, about other people, and been completely wrong and not taken other people's feelings and what they might be going through into consideration.

It was not all about me. Even when it was just the dog and me, it obviously was not always about me.

Another reason I was emotional was because I was agreeing with her and seeing all the beauty around us and how good it was for both of us to be out together enjoying that wonderful walk on that joyous day.

I was also emotional because she/we had truly rounded a corner.

She was walking and looking around and sniffing, almost like normal. Life was grand again, and I along with Ciccina, could smell again and pay attention to sounds again, and walk around like we owned the town. The only thing we couldn't do was smile like we used to.

I was beginning to think that that Ciccina's face was going to be crooked forever. I didn't know what made me think that, it had only been a couple days since the accident, and it already looked better than it did immediately afterwards. Could I be that much in a hurry? Could I be that ungrateful for everything that had changed for the better? Could I only be focusing on what was not good?

All the while I was having my conflicting thoughts in my head, Ciccina had walked us around the whole block. When we got back around to the stairs, she was ready to go up them and back inside. Before leaning down to pick her up and carry her up the stairs, that time I stopped, watched and waited. I waited to see if she was going to be looking at me for help or if she was going to try and climb them on her own.

With only the slightest hesitation, initially, Ciccina put one paw out in front of her and hoisted her body up the first step. She then paused as she had done coming down the stairs, and then did it again. Step by step she scaled each step on her own. This time, however, I not only remembered to not worry, or wonder if she was going to make it, but instead I cheered her on. I gave her praise. I told her she could do it, and in the end, she did it.

When we finally got inside, the rest of our day was still ahead of us. Ciccina ate, with a little help from her friend, then we did energy work, we listened to music, were surrounded by crystals, incense was going, and it actually was quite beautiful. That was the kind of thing and the kind of time I never took for myself. As much as I loved music, I rarely played it at my place. Between phone calls and the music I would be working on, there wasn't time to be playing it in the background, in my way of thinking at the time. I loved the smell of certain types of incense, and though I had it, I rarely lit it. Taking time for revitalizing my energy or even just resting and "doing nothing," was something that I had not done in a long time.

I would consider my performance travels my vacations. As much as I enjoyed performing and working, they were not the same as a vacation. Rarely did I have time to myself, with the obligations of meet and greets and rehearsals and dinner parties, etc. These moments with Ciccina were making me think how much I needed to refresh myself every once in awhile.

Of course, though it seemed like I was doing "nothing" as far as I was doing less "work," I was "working" on Ciccina, so I was still working. But somehow while "healing" her, I was also "healing" me. At the end of the day, it was time for bed again. That day had been a day of reawakening and reemerging in so many ways. Ciccina had reemerged on the "world scene."

I was starting to feel like I could reemerge too. On an average day, I spoke to many people, from business calls to calls with friends, I was always talking to someone or meeting someone or going to meetings. Over those past few days, I had stopped speaking to anyone all together. I even didn't call Dorothy back after that conversation in which she told me to breathe, go within, tune in, and listen for the answers, and I would know what to do. She also said a lot of other things that I just couldn't take in at the moment. Part of the reason I wasn't calling anyone was because I wasn't getting too much work done, though I tried, because I was spending so much time with Ciccina, so I needed the time to work.

Again, another reason I wasn't talking to anyone was because I didn't want to tell anyone what was going on. I didn't want to chance anyone telling me it wasn't possible. I just didn't want that in my mind. I also didn't want to chance anyone telling me that I was crazy. I knew what I was doing was not "normal," but I also knew that I wasn't making it up. I was certain that I was getting messages and communicating with Ciccina and the proof was at that moment staring me in the face. Everything happening the way it happened those past couple of days could not have been a coincidence. I was sure of that.

I began to wonder if some aspects, or all aspects of what I had been doing and going through with Ciccina was actually "normal," and I never knew it, or society didn't know it. I wondered if maybe there was ever a time, or a Country, tribe or civilization that lived in ways that espoused and incorporated that kind of energy healing and way of being in their daily life.

I remembered that years ago I had read a non-fiction book titled, "Mutant Message Down Under," in which the author, Marlo Morgan tells a story of an experience that happened to her while on a walkabout with Australian aborigines. During the trip, one of the members of the tribe tripped from "accidentally" stepping into a hole and broke her leg. The tribe gathered around the injured member and laid hands on her and prayed.

As I recalled, the injured tribe woman was able to walk again quickly, like within the same day, as if nothing had ever happened. According to Marlo the leg had visibly and obviously been broken, but even if it had only been a sprain or a twisted ankle, that healing period would have been a significantly fast healing time. As interesting as this was to me, what was more interesting was that Marlo went on to write, that unbeknownst to her, the tribe wanted to show her how they were able to heal themselves quickly, and energetically. She wrote that the night before the "accident" happened, the tribe members had decided that they would show her that "miracle" healing the next day. And in order to show her, one of the tribe members would have to have an "accident."

According to her, each tribe member volunteered to allow themselves to be the one who was injured. They collectively agreed to "let" the "accident" happen to the one who would be the best one for the "job." The next day, no one knew which one of them would have the "accident," but they all knew one of them would, and that the injured one would heal right before Marlo's eyes, for Marlo's edification.

If Marlo's story was true, could this have been exactly what was going on with Ciccina and I. After all, Dorothy had said that I was going to learn a lesson from Ciccina before I found her another home. Does this kind of stuff happen all the time? And just like

Marlo, if the tribe members had not told her, she wouldn't have known that they had planned it. Do things happen around us for our benefit sometimes? And are some of the things that happen supposed to be answers to our questions? Or worse, are some of the things that happen around us because of us, and our thoughts? I say worse, because especially in that situation with Ciccina, I had noticed that so many of my thoughts were negative. And if thoughts were things, holding on to negative thoughts might have led to some of the negative things which happened in my life.

I took all of that to heart and was really trying to expand my thinking beyond anything that I ever thought possible before. I thought, maybe I should call Dorothy.

At that point, it was too late in the night to call anyone however, and it was time for Ciccina's "energy bath." We also had to set our goal for the next day. I was feeling like I was running out of goals to set for her, Ciccina had come so far. Sure, her physical energy wasn't what it was, but she walked and ate and drank and pooped and everything was almost normal, except her face.

Something said to me, "let's set a goal for her face to be back to normal by tomorrow." Upon having that thought, I immediately attributed that to my ego and my vanity to have "my dog" be pretty again and I wiped that thought from my mind. I felt like I was testing my "wizard abilities." In other words, "let's do something outrageous and see how good 'I' am," which would have been completely ego driven. As far as vanity was concerned, my dog was beautiful and alive and that was the most important thing of all.

That thought about Ciccina being beautiful just as she was and alive being the most important thing made me stop and wonder if I had always thought that way about dogs, or people, or better yet, myself. I brushed that question out of my mind, for fear of what the answer would be, and I went back to trying to think of a goal for the next day.

Again, the thought of Ciccina's face going back to normal popped into my mind. I was actually afraid to think of that because I didn't know how to fix that. Of course, I didn't know how to fix anything else, and I certainly wasn't taking credit for having fixed anything, although I certainly did believe that I had helped.

For some reason the face was a tough one for me. I had a hard time believing it could go back to normal. Not only that, my ego didn't want to "wish" for something that might not have come true. For a moment, I had a thought that went something like this, "If I ask for her face to come back to normal, and it doesn't, it will ruin 'my' record of everything else happening just as 'I' thought it would each day prior."

I thought I was doing great with not needing for "my" dog to be "pretty," and felt I had come a long way to that way of thinking, and there I was again feeling like I was being asked to take two more steps forward.

Ciccina was staring me in the eyes as if to say, "You're getting it kid." And as I stared back, I couldn't help but think that she was taunting me, "Go ahead, since you did all of this, make my face go back to normal!" It was laughable, but I wasn't laughing, even though I could have used a laugh at that point. "I didn't do it," I exclaimed in my head, "I couldn't do it." I insisted that it wasn't me that made the miracles happen. I knew at the very least that if they did involve me, that there was something else at play there much bigger than me.

I caught myself in my head again judging myself and denying myself possibilities. At least I was no longer in fear and anxiety. That was a good step in the right direction for me. I was also not in worry mode, as I usually got into before big trips and performances. As I cleared my mind the judgment of myself and of the situation went away quickly enough. But the thought of Ciccina's face returning to 100% didn't go away.

I tried to get rid of it but it just wouldn't go away, so I knew I had to work with it. Maybe I just didn't believe it would happen, or at least so soon, or without the help of a cast or something. Maybe I didn't want to be disappointed if it didn't happen. Maybe it was just my ego, again. I stopped my thoughts again and asked myself the following question, "What was the real truth of what I wanted?"

I didn't have to think long about it. By then I had been so connected to my true, raw, deep down inside feelings, that the answers to questions were coming up easier and quicker. The answer came up and out quickly, that I truly wanted Ciccina's face healed 100%, period. I wouldn't love her any less if it didn't happen. I wouldn't feel like a failure if it didn't happen. Knowing my ego was in check and that this was about Ciccina, I was no longer afraid to ask or to set that as a goal.

I turned to Ciccina and with confidence and conviction I said to her, "Ciccina, tomorrow morning your face is going to be back to normal!" "Sarai bella again," I said to her in half Italian and half English, like I often spoke to her, meaning, "You'll be beautiful again."

Even though my voice sounded confident and convinced, deep down inside I was still trying my best to believe that was even possible. I also was trying my best to not be attached to the outcome and yet visualize the outcome at the same time. How that could happen in one night was beyond me, but then so was everything else that had happened in those past few days. All of what had happened had been so magical and mystical and supernatural, that at times I wondered if I was just going to wake up one of those mornings, and find out that it had been just a dream; like in the "Wizard of Oz." But each morning I kept waking up, and finding that I was still "not in Kansas."

The next morning, I awoke, much like the other mornings, in anticipation of yet another miracle. Only, as far as Ciccina's recovery, that miracle would be the last. With much excitement, I turned around to look at Ciccina and to see her newly "perfect" face. I was surprised to not see the face that I expected to see. In fact, I did not see Ciccina's face at all, or her body for that matter. I had gotten so used to seeing her sitting on her pillow staring at me each morning that I had forgotten what it was like for her to have the ability to walk and the will to walk about the whole place.

Had I thought about it, this could have been a goal too, her feeling free to roam at her will and not have to just sit on the pillow until I woke up. But assuming everything else happened, that would have been a given.

"Ciccina," I called as I got out of bed, "Where are you bella?"

Before I had time to walk out of my room she walked toward me waddling, that waddle that accompanied her wagging tail. Her body was straighter and she walked much more confidently. That was another thing to cheer about. She came when she heard me call her and that was wonderful too.

"There you are. How are you this morning, huh?" How are you?"

Seeing her up and about took me out of my recent morning routine of going directly to the crystals and giving her an energy bath etc., and brought me back for a moment to how things used to be. I used to get up and go to greet Ciccina good morning in the office, because she didn't sleep in my bedroom, at that time. Then I walked over to the computer, turned it on and shuffled some papers around on my desk while waiting for it to boot up. I'd check a few things, like my schedule for the day, and then Ciccina and I would take a walk, have breakfast and spend some time together.

That morning I was still planning on doing energy work on her, but having been knocked into how things used be, by not finding Ciccina in my room, I started to make my way toward my office to do my old morning ritual. I was so far into, "I better get things done before I have to leave for my trip," mode, that I had forgotten all about our goal.

I turned on my computer and started to shuffle some papers around and got engrossed in doing something at my desk, as per previously normal. And also, as per previously normal, since Ciccina had come into my life, we had gotten into an old habit, she would follow me into my office. Eventually she hovered near my desk to watch me, for an occasional petting, and sometimes to jump on my lap. That morning was much like that, only I wasn't paying attention to it at all. Instead of following me up to my desk, Ciccina stood at the entrance of the office staring at me. As I worked, I felt like someone was staring at me and that it wasn't the usual stare. It was piercing. I felt it hard, and I looked up.

Of course, it was Ciccina, standing at the door staring as if to say, "Hey, what happened? Where's my attention this morning?"

She was right to be thrown off a bit since I had been focusing all my mornings on her and she deserved my attention, period, every morning, on healing days and normal days.

"Hey!" I smiled and said to her out loud, "Look at you how beautiful you are!" not really taking note of anything different in particular, just making small talk with her as I used to do, buying time, until I could drop what I was doing and could give her some more attention.

"Ciccina!" I shouted as I leaped from my desk chair, "Look at you, you're all better!" I ran over to her not sure if she looked fine because I was looking at her from the angle from where I was sitting, or if that morning had given rise to another miracle, another goal met.

"Let me look at you Ciccina, let me see!" I rambled on as I approached her excitedly. Upon reaching her, I gently grabbed her face and moved it from side to side. My speech then became slow and methodical, "You are amazing! I can't believe you! How did you do this? You did it! You really did it!" I kept repeating in disbelief. I couldn't believe it. I knew that I should believe it and that that was exactly everything that we had been working on, but I had never seen anything like that and to me it was still unbelievable, even though it happened pretty much in front of my eyes. It was a miracle.

"I asked for it, and I got it." came the thought. Then came the next thought, "Would Ciccina's face have been fine this morning had I not asked for it to be so and had Ciccina and I not set it as a goal the night before?"

I wasn't sure of the exact answer, but I was sure that that was not a coincidence. In fact, none of them had been coincidences. Each morning, the specific things that we had put attention on the night before, as we set our goals, came true. It baffled me that it not only happened, but that it happened so quickly, and that it happened when we asked it to happen. For example, the face could have come back to normal days ago, but instead we had put attention on the eating, and that happened, and the walking, or the wagging of the tail, and then they happened. The fact that they all happened, and that they all happened within four days was a miracle in itself. But the fact that they happened as we willed them to happen was blowing my mind even more.

I looked for "rational" explanations. I thought, maybe I was tuned into what the natural progression, or possible progression, of healing was, and I just called it in that way. Maybe Ciccina was tuned into how she was going to go about her healing and she was projecting on to me what we were to do next. Maybe it was a little of both or a lot of other things too. I wanted to contemplate and try and figure that out. I wanted to call Dorothy and say, "You were right."

I wanted to celebrate Ciccina, and the miracle. And at that very moment, Ciccina was still sitting right in front of me looking up at me with her beautiful face and beautiful smile. I turned to her and said, "Ciccina, I'm so proud of you!" "I can't believe you." "Look at you." I couldn't stop saying those things to her over and over.

That day Ciccina walked a lot farther, ate a lot more, on her own, wagged her tail a lot more and her face looked almost 100%. Truthfully, her face was back to normal but she wasn't really smiling like she used to. Her energy was also still low and it was reflected in the look on her face.

It had been a miraculous day, and in some way it had seemed pretty much like a new normal day. But there was nothing normal about that day. Even though for the rest of the day, Ciccina and I did some normal things, and started to go back to our "normal" daily life, we were both two very different beings. On the one hand, here was a dog that by all accounts had been dead and on that day was walking as if nothing had happened. On the other hand, there was a man who was a wreck only days before and days later he was confidently "co-creating miracles" like he had never done before. What had happened? What had happened to Ciccina? What had happened to me?

As night fell, I decided it would be good to still set another goal for Ciccina's recovery. The only things I could think of was her overall energy and her bark. Her energy had obviously been down and I had not heard her bark since the "accident." I knew she could bark because of all the yelping she had done. I had also heard her whine a little, moan and make noises in her sleep. But I had not heard her bark.

What I thought would be a good testing of her energy and hence a good goal was to see her do what she used to do at the door every time I suggested we were going to go for a walk. I would say, "Do you want to go bye, bye?" The next thing that would happen would be that Ciccina would start barking and jumping up and down, and propping herself up against the front door with her front paws. She had gotten a little bit excited in these past couple days, but not nearly as much as before. Her tail had started to wag when I would mention going bye, bye, but there was no barking and no propping herself up on the door.

This was what I visualized as I gave her her final energy bath that night. I told her exactly what I was going to do and what she was going to do and I told her, that that was the way she was going to show me everything was finally all okay.

The next morning after waking up and petting her and getting ready, I stood at the door with the leash in my hand and I waited until she pranced up to me and looked up into my eyes. I then gave the signal for all joy to break loose and I said the magic words.

"For the big prize Ciccina, for the miracle that you are, tell me that you are healed." I thought to myself, "Show me your excitement!" "Do you want to go bye, bye?"

I watched in pure elation as Ciccina jumped up, propped herself at the front door and barked as if to say, "WE DID IT!" "WE WON!"

23 I GOT TO GET READY TO GO, AND SO DOES CICCINA

I was a happier person than I had been in a long time. I could not have been happier with the results of the past few days. After Ciccina barked we both ran, not walked, outside, down the stairs and she started running as I started jogging down the block. I jogged and jumped and Ciccina pranced and hopped right alongside me. When we both tired out we started walking the rest of the way.

If it had been up to Ciccina, we would have walked ten times around the block, she had so much energy. But this time it was me who steered her around to head us back home. She was busy smelling and looking around and barking and playing and doing her thing and surely couldn't have understood why we had to go back.

I understood her very well, and I couldn't have been happier for her and was right there with her. I matched her energy and the two of us were very tuned-in together. But what was going on in my mind were two things. Ciccina had barely been able to walk just a couple days before and I didn't want her overexerting herself. I knew that she knew what she was doing, and at the same time, I knew we still had the whole day ahead of us and we could do a walk again later. I thought it was a good idea to break it up a little bit. The other thing that was on my mind was my upcoming trip, performances, and finding the right home for Ciccina in what was only a couple of days. If I couldn't find her a good home in the time remaining, I had decided that I wanted to at least find her a good place to stay while I was away for a week.

Besides all that, I hadn't even arranged my music, packed my bags, rehearsed with the musical director, etc., etc. I had been in a time warp, and it all seemed like a dream, a nightmare, and a dream at the same time. But I knew it had been real and I couldn't wait to tell everyone about it once I was back in the "regular" world. But the reality of the moment was that I didn't have time to tell anyone anything, I had another kind of work to do.

For the sake of finding Ciccina a good home, or a temporary place to stay for a week, the first person I called was Laura. I told Laura that I was in a dilemma and asked if she could help. As always, she answered, "Anything honey, what's up?" without even knowing what I was going to ask her.

"I have to go out of town to perform for a week, in a just few days and I don't have anyone to leave Ciccina with," I explained.

"Oh, honey, geez, I can't believe it. You know how I have been since I lost my little ones? Well, for the first time, in all this time, I actually allowed myself to help out another friend and allowed myself to open up my home to my friend's two dogs. She's going out of town too. Oh, honey, I'm sorry, I can't take her." She continued, "One of them is a really big dog and it's hard for me to even control him actually, I wouldn't want to scare your little one. God knows she's been through enough as it is."

Laura didn't even know what had happened on the evening of the Fourth of July. By saying that, she was referring to having been lost or abandoned on the street etc.

Laura continued without giving me a moment to interject. In her sincere desire to help, she was looking for a solution in her mind. "Let me see if anyone in my community of friends wants to take care of your dog while you're away," she said.

"Thank you Laura, I don't know what else to do at this point," I responded, and we hung up soon after.

When I got off the phone I looked down at Ciccina and had a thought. I found it strange how Ciccina and I could "bring her back from the dead," but we couldn't find her a home. I would have thought that this would have been the easier of the two things to do. I also had the thought that if somehow Ciccina and the "accident" were parts of a grand, master plan, then surely the plan would include a home for Ciccina too, after all that had transpired.

After calling Laura, I called Dorothy. Not that Dorothy would know anyone that could help since she lived in San Diego and I in Los Angeles, but Dorothy had been right about everything all along. I wanted to check in with her. Dorothy was the one who told me that I would find Ciccina a home after I learned a lesson from her. If Dorothy had been right about that too, then I hoped and trusted that I had learned all the lessons I needed to, for two reasons. I hated to think that Ciccina had gone through all that she had gone through, for me to learn a lesson. But if that were exactly what happened, then I wanted the lesson time for Ciccina to have been over. I couldn't have imagined anything else happening to Ciccina. Secondly, I wanted so much to find Ciccina a good home, so, if I had learned my lesson, then according to Dorothy, a good home for Ciccina was forthcoming.

As I started to dial Dorothy, I realized that I hadn't spoken to her since that day she told so many things that I didn't want to hear. It had been a while since our last conversation and so much had happened. So much of what Dorothy said had come to pass. I had no idea how she did that, but I was hoping she would be right about the last part too, the part about finding Ciccina a home.

Once getting her on the phone, I told Dorothy how Ciccina had recovered 100% and how everything that we had talked about had come true. I told her how I had put her Chakra Box to good use and how much that box had come in handy. I thanked her for the box again and more importantly, for her support, encouragement and guidance. I don't think I would have been able to go through what I went through without her wisdom, as much as I didn't want to hear it at first.

Dorothy couldn't have been more pleased. She told me that ever since she met me she had been working with me, helping me activate my abilities to connect and reawaken to my power, and had been working on accelerating my recognition of my abilities and my mission in this lifetime. I hadn't known Dorothy very long, but with Dorothy, it seemed that just when I was warming up to something she had told me prior, she would hit me with something else that I didn't want to hear, or couldn't hear or understand at that moment.

That was yet another example. I did not understand what she was saying, much less be ready to take all that she said in. But Dorothy wasn't done. She told me that she had told the story of Ciccina to a couple fellow spiritual healers and that she and they all decided I was ready for the next level. She went on to say that when I got back from performing out of town, they were setting up a private crash course for me in "Energetic Alchemy" so I could learn exactly what I did with Ciccina, and learn how to do more of it.

I wasn't sure at the time about all that she was saying. As far as I was concerned, I thought I was done with the healing and miracle stuff. I was hoping that had been a one-time thing. Evidently, not, according to Dorothy. I came to learn that in Dorothy's world, this was an "everyday" kind of thing. In her words, "if we are lucky enough to have the gifts and recognize them, then we must share them for the good of humanity"

I was humbled by the thought that she and two of her colleagues would think so highly of me and my "abilities," to take a weekend and dedicate it to teaching me the ins and outs of "Energetic Alchemy," whatever that was. I knew "Energetic Alchemy" was a course that Dorothy had developed and it dealt with energy and healing. That much I knew. But in my mind, I had visions of the Hogwarts school that Harry Potter went to, wherein I would learn how to use a magic wand and make things fly. Of course this had nothing to do with what she was proposing, but I did enjoy the thought.

I thanked Dorothy and told her that I would want to talk more about it, but that at the moment I had to worry about finding Ciccina a home.

"Don't 'worry' about it. Worrying only makes it worse," Dorothy said as she interrupted me and stopped me in mid-sentence to correct me. "Put energy on it," she continued.

"Put energy on what?" I questioned.

"Put energy on finding Ciccina a home," she responded.

"I am putting energy on finding Ciccina a home," I quickly responded. "I've called Laura and..."

"No, that's not what I mean," she said, "I mean energy, like you used to heal Ciccina. Put the same energy on finding her a home."

"Oh, that's interesting," was all I could say at that point. Only days before I didn't know what she meant. A week or so later, I knew exactly what she meant because I had done it, only I wasn't getting how it applied in that situation. I could tell that what Dorothy was telling me was making me stretch my thinking some more. I was being asked to take another step forward and do "energy" work in another context.

As if everything else that had happened throughout the week wasn't weird enough, the concept that I was trying to grasp with Dorothy on the phone, was weird to me. I had never done things like what had happened, but somehow I had done it and it was a part of me, in a sense. The energy on finding Ciccina a home, that, seemed weird to me, I had never done anything like that either, at least not that I could remember. That was obviously not something I was taught growing up, in school, not in church, and not at the University or in my previous corporate job for that matter. It wasn't something people did, or was it? I had started reading books and listening to tapes over the past prior years that talked about power, the mind, and thinking etc. Was that what all those books and tapes were referring to?

Maybe I had been asking for the awakening, activation, and acceleration as Dorothy called it, for quite some time? For years I had acquired, accumulated and read books and listened to tapes. I watched videos and sought out as much esoteric knowledge on the subjects that I could. Maybe I wasn't understanding what I was reading. Maybe that which happened was all outlined in the books, in a way. Maybe it was all there? Maybe the answers were there too?

That night, I decided to give Ciccina an energy bath. But it turned out to be different. It wasn't like the ones we had done the days and nights prior. That one wasn't focused on her body, it was focused on her life, her future, her new home and new family. I didn't use the Chakra Box or a pendulum, but I did grab a crystal and held on to it, for "energy," or to have something to hold on to, I wasn't sure which, or both, maybe?

I started saying to her, out loud, while I "put energy on her," with my hands, "Ciccina, tomorrow we are going to find you a beautiful home, with a beautiful family who loves you, and knows how to take good care of you. You are going to have a nice yard to play in, and good food and you will be so happy. I promise you, I'll come to visit every once in awhile. You'll be happy there. It will be the best possible place for you, ever!"

Soon after doing that, we went to bed; me in my bed, and Ciccina on her pillow, in my bedroom. When morning came I was anxiously awaiting Laura's call. I went about my morning telling Ciccina that we had found her a beautiful home and that I couldn't wait to introduce her to her new family. I was either saying that as a positive affirmation or I was really thinking that it was a done deal. After all, Laura was on it, and she knew many people, and many dog lovers, and I knew she loved Ciccina and I, and would do everything she could to make it happen. Ciccina seemed oblivious to the whole thing. She wasn't worried. What did she have to be worried about? She could cross a street and meet me. Then she could cross the same street months later, get run over and heal herself. Surely the next phase of her life was going to be just as magical and just as perfect, with hopefully no accidents.

"If only I could live that way," I heard myself think in my head! What an interesting thought. I was envious of my dog's life. Well, not my dog's life, per se, but her way of being. In fact, in a way, she had taught me "how to be." She had shown me, for the most part, how she did it. Had I not learned that, in all that time?

"Yes!" I had learned a lot and though there was certainly more for me to learn from her, I knew for certain that Ciccina was ready to go on to her next adventure, and I on to mine.

There it was, another knowing. Interesting how up until that moment, I had not had that "knowing." I had wondered at times, "Is this my dog like people say?" even though I knew I couldn't have kept her. Again, I remembered Dorothy saying to me that I had something to learn from the dog and that she would be my dog until such time that I learned it, and then I would find her the perfect home and family.

I had developed certainty around the Ciccina and the learning situation. I knew that I had finally learned what I needed to learn, and on some level, evidently wanted, to learn. Whatever it was I was supposed to learn from Ciccina, I had learned it. I recognized that our time together had been so very important and I wouldn't have traded it. I was grateful for her having been in my life, for all of the experiences, and for all of the learnings. I knew that the time had come for Ciccina to be in a new home.

The phone rang, and startled me out of my moment of contemplation, understanding and gratitude. It was Laura. "I found Ciccina the perfect home," she was excited to tell me. "I am so happy for her. This is a friend of mine who has a beautiful home in the Hollywood Hills with a big yard for Ciccina to run around in. She'll be really happy there. And she wants her, not just to take care of this week, she wants to keep her!"

While I was hearing Laura tell me all that good news, the finality of it all was sinking in. I started to wonder what it would be like waking up and not finding Ciccina looking at me. What would it be like not having to take her for her morning "sensory" walks? What would it be like not having her waddle and bark and watch me?

"Honey, are you there?" Laura called out over the phone, once again taking me out of my moment of contemplation.

"I'm sorry, thank you so much, that sounds perfect." I quickly responded. As I reflected on what she had just said, I started putting pieces together. Laura lives in the Hollywood Hills. Laura has a big beautiful yard. And Laura kept referring to her "friend" as a she. Well, Laura was a she. I happily came to the conclusion, and exclaimed in my head, "Laura's taking Ciccina!"

I started thinking how perfect that was going to be and that I had known it all along. I just knew Ciccina was Laura's dog. I started thinking about what it would be like to go visit Laura and get to see Ciccina any time I wanted. Laura was so great with dogs and I knew Ciccina would be so well taken care of. Laura missed her two little dogs so much, I was happy for her, that she would have a dog again, and that Ciccina would be her dog.

"Honey, what's wrong with you? What's going on?" Laura asked on the other end of the phone, again, startling me out of my contemplation.

"So you're really taking her?" I responded with excitement.

"No, I just told you, I have a friend who is taking her. Are you okay?" she asked. "I told you I can't take her right now cause I'm dog sitting two dogs already. I would have watched her only while you were gone. Anyway, you told me you wanted me to help you find her a home. Well, this is it, this friend of mine wants to keep her. Isn't it great?"

In her retelling how this had all gone down, Laura had sent her friend a picture, and told her all about Ciccina. Her friend supposedly said that that was just the kind of dog she wanted. According to Laura she was a very nice person and she assured me that she wouldn't have suggested her if she didn't think she would take great care of Ciccina, because, in her words, "Ciccina is very special to me too."

"I'm sorry, the way you described your friend, I thought it was you. And yes, thank you so much, it all sounds perfect. I'm excited for Ciccina," I responded.

Laura proceeded to give me her friend's name and number and

told me to call her right away because she was expecting my call.

I thanked Laura again, hung up the phone, and then took a moment to look at Ciccina, and said, "Well, we did it, we manifested it," before I made the call.

The lady was really pleasant on the phone and she sounded excited about the prospect of having a new dog. She was at work so she couldn't speak for long, but she told me to call her at home the next evening at which time she would give me her address and have me drop off Ciccina. I was a little leery of waiting until the following day, because that next night was cutting it close. I had an early flight the morning after and had lots to do still to get ready.

Though I cherished the extra time with Ciccina, I worried if I would get everything done before I left. Nonetheless, it was what it was, and I was assured that she would take Ciccina. I was happy for Ciccina that she had finally found her home and new family.

The next day, I frantically packed and did everything I could do to get ready while all the while I took glances at Ciccina. As usual, I petted her any chance I got and reassured her verbally that it was a good thing and everything that we had agreed on and manifested. I had the feeling Ciccina wasn't convinced. But everything up till that point had gone according to "plan," whether we knew the plan or not. To look at Ciccina, one could hardly argue with success. Why would that go any differently?

I called the lady on her office number in the afternoon just to confirm my bringing Ciccina to her that evening, but I had to leave her a message on her answering machine. I knew she was working so that shouldn't have bothered me that she didn't pick up the phone. I figured if I didn't hear from her during office hours, I would call her at home afterwards and make arrangements then, as originally planned anyway.

Even so, maybe it was my worries coming in to play, but something did not feel right about her not picking up the phone. I didn't know why, because people don't pick up the phone lots of times. I didn't always pick up the phone myself, why would it bother me that this person didn't pick up the phone. People are busy, people are in meetings, people are on other calls, there are lots of reasons why people don't pick up phones. There was no reason to worry, no cause for alarm, yet I felt uneasy. Nevertheless, the woman was a professional and a friend of Laura's and surely wouldn't have blown me off. Besides, she assured me she really wanted Ciccina.

Something inside me still said that it wasn't going to work out. Was that my ego, or my fears coming up? Could I have possibly "connected" and could possibly have been right thanks to my new found connection with "knowings?" I wasn't sure how to tell whether it was one thing or another. But I knew for sure that time would tell, and then I would know.

True, time would tell, but time was the one thing I didn't have much of. If for some reason the lady didn't call back or I didn't connect with her, then I didn't know what I would do. What was I supposed to do with Ciccina? Whether I was having old worries or fear or actual "knowings," I wasn't sure, but I called Laura just in case.

Laura assured me that her friend was an upfront person. She went on to say that she was a dog lover, had a dog already and wanted another small one that got along with other dogs, and just raved over the picture and said she wanted Ciccina.

Unbeknownst to me, Laura was also feeling something was not quite right after receiving my phone call, so Laura called her friend herself after getting off the phone with me. She too ended up leaving her a message and then called me to let me know that her friend must be out of the office because she didn't even respond to her. But she was sure we would both hear from her.

Well, hear from her I didn't. When it was after office hours it was time to call her at home. So I did, only to get another answering machine answering my call. I left a message letting her know that I had to have Ciccina settled into her home, that very night, since I was leaving out of town on an early flight in the morning.

Having had no return phone call, I waited an hour, and then called back. I got the answering machine again. Again I left a message, only this time I pleaded for her to call me back. In my message I asked her to return the call ASAP even if she had changed her mind so I would know in as much time in advance if I had to make other arrangements. Of course, other arrangements were not an option in my mind or a possibility, as I saw it.

In my mind there weren't many options left and as I hung up the phone I looked at Ciccina and I said, "Where did we go wrong? It's got to work out, we manifested it. We put the energy on it and everything, right?"

In an act of what I think was more desperation than enlightenment, I looked at Ciccina and said almost the exact same words I said to her only a week or so before on that Fourth of July night. "Ciccina, I know you can find yourself a home, I just know it. I can help you, but you have to want it. You can do it; I know you can. You just got to. I believe in you!"

My new "knowing" was that everything would be perfect somehow, but in my mind I was a wreck. The situation was odd and yet it felt very normal to me. Being a wreck in my mind was my modus operandi, but since Ciccina, I had turned over a new leaf. Ciccina and I had worked on that and I didn't want to go back to the way I was before. Ciccina had showed me a new way to be, live, and do. I didn't like being a wreck, I liked it when I just "knew," like, once I really knew what I knew, I knew Ciccina was going to be okay, and she was.

As time passed, I became more and more a wreck, even though I "knew" everything was going to work out. It seemed like a better place to be, than just being a wreck and not knowing if things would work out, but for me it was not better enough. In my anxiety, I called Dorothy and told her my dilemma. I explained to her everything that was going wrong. She chuckled under her breath and caught herself because she didn't want to sound unsympathetic, "Honey, I know what you're saying to me, but 'they' keep telling me its time and that it's going to be better than you think."

There was that "they" again. I still wasn't sure who "they" were, but I couldn't argue, because "they" had been right about everything else up until that point. For all I knew, "they" could have been the ones talking or guiding me through this whole process all that time. But what if "their" sense of timing was different than my timing. Did "they" know or understand that I had a plane to catch in less than 12 hours? What was I supposed to do with Ciccina? Could "they" take care of her?

Unfortunately, most of this conversation which could have been had in my head was actually being had out loud, with Dorothy on the phone. I wasn't trying to be disrespectful to Dorothy or "them." I was just trying to handle the situation as best I could and remain calm, but I could tell I wasn't handling it well.

In an aha moment, it came to me that someone or something definitely had truly orchestrated everything that had gone on and was going on. I do believe in a Higher Power, call it God, call it, The Universe, call it All That Is, call it Energy, I believe in it.

Though I had thought about it before, I finally came to believe and really see that I could not have planned any of what had transpired between Ciccina and I in all those months. I had come to see how everything that had happened, whether it was intended for my benefit or not, did work out for my benefit, or at least that is how I was looking at it, and eventually for Ciccina's too.

I was seeing how much I had learned and grown and most of all trusted in something greater than I in all that time. I had come to see how I allowed and resigned myself to be guided. Something else was at work, and if that moment was the way it was, it was that way for my benefit, or if not, that at the very least, it would turn out to be so, if I just went with it.

I recalled Dorothy's words, when I asked her what to do about Ciccina's recovery, she said, "breathe, connect and listen."

"Breathe, connect and listen," I reminded myself. After hanging up the phone with Dorothy, I took a moment to quiet myself in order to breathe, connect and listen. But unfortunately, the moment did not last long. Not that I knew how long it was supposed to last. Maybe it did last exactly as long as it was supposed to last? In my mind I should have "meditated" for an hour or something. But Dorothy never said meditate, and she never told me how long it was supposed to take for me to get an answer.

And an answer came. In actuality, I didn't know if I had gotten an answer or if my panicking mind needed to call the lady again. But I felt like I had to. So, I called the home number one more time. And that time, someone answered. It was a man, and he was whispering on the phone. I wasn't sure who he was or why he was whispering, but I was so happy to have someone answer the phone that I didn't think much of it and I didn't really care.

I asked for the lady of the house and he told me that she was asleep. That would explain the whispering. I told him who I was and that I had spoken to her about her adopting my dog. He told me he had heard the messages, to which I was relieved, but that he had not heard his wife mention that she was adopting a dog.

That surprised me but I didn't let that stop me. "So, could I speak with your wife then about this?" I persisted.

"As I mentioned, she's asleep after a very difficult day and because she hadn't mentioned this, I am going to assume you talked to someone else but it wasn't my wife." he adamantly said.

I couldn't believe what I was hearing. I was stunned. I felt as if the blood had rushed out of my head and was leaving my body. What could be the meaning of that? Who could assume I was lying about something like that? Who wouldn't wake up his wife and why wouldn't he? She couldn't have been asleep very long, I had called only an hour or so prior. Why had she not mentioned it to him? What was wrong with those people? What was going on?

My mind was racing a mile a minute and I wanted to be angry with the person on the phone, but I heard myself calmly say nonetheless, "I don't understand why this is happening, but if I can't convince you to wake your wife, then there is nothing I can do. Good night."

"Good night?" I wanted to say something different, something not nearly as pleasant, something not as "good." But that was not my modus operandi and certainly not after what I had been through with Ciccina and all that I had learned.

I felt mistreated, not believed, not respected, deceived, and so much more. In mid-thought, I caught myself and I realized that I had taken all that had transpired on the phone personally, that my ego was hurt and I was angry, pure and simple. Though it was all justifiable in my mind, if I had learned anything in the past few months, I had learned that I had to be open to the bigger picture whatever that might be. There had to be a bigger picture that I wasn't seeing, and in the end it would be good for all involved maybe even better than I could have imagined.

"Please God, let there be another perspective! Help me see it!" I exclaimed out loud.

I had no time or patience to breathe, connect and listen, I had to call Laura right away. Laura answered the phone sounding like she had been asleep. It had gotten much later than I thought, which might have been a good thing that I had not realized the time, otherwise I might have gotten myself in even more of a panic and I also might not have called Laura for fear of waking her up.

I tried to disguise my panic with Laura and sound as calm as I could, though I could tell she knew something was up when she answered the phone with "What happened?" I would have thought that she would have assumed that I was calling her to thank her and to tell her it all went well. But her "what happened?" was not an excited "what happened?" it was a "what went wrong?" kind of "what happened?"

"Well, I called the lady and her husband answered the phone and told me that his wife was sleeping and that he wasn't going to wake her up because she never mentioned adopting a dog to him," I recounted, without even taking a breath.

"What? I can't believe this! This is not like her! What?" she repeated, not believing the turn of events.

"Oh my God, Honey, what are you going to do?" she quickly asked.

"I don't know," I responded with my heart back in my throat like on the first day I met Ciccina. When I met her she didn't have a home and months later there she was, without a home again. I had only wanted to do good for that dog, and I was becoming overwhelmed with all the "bad," as I was seeing it, again, at that moment. I wanted so much for that precious dog to have the home she deserved and right at that moment she didn't have it. I felt like I had failed her, like I hadn't "planned her life right."

I had gone "there" again. It was a place I was used to going in my mind, when things weren't going quite like I wanted them to. I went into shaming myself, blaming myself, and looking only at things as failure. In that moment, I was ignoring any of the good, or in that case, the miraculous and unbelievably amazing things that had happened. Little did I know, that the more I went "there," the harder it was for things to go the way I wanted them too, because, I was putting "energy" on what I didn't want.

"Don't worry honey," once again Laura interrupted my worrisome thoughts, "bring her here."

"What? You said you couldn't keep her because of the two other dogs, and one of them is a big dog." I questioned.

"I know honey, but this is an emergency, what else are you going to do?" she responded.

I started to answer her, but she immediately came back with, "I'll keep her in my room with me. Ciccina and I will have a great time, and we'll stay away from the other dogs, unless they play nice in the morning. She'll be fine, bring her over. Are you going to come over right now?"

"I'll be right there." I answered as a little bit of excitement started to come back into my voice.

"Bring a shirt of yours that has your smell on it and whatever she sleeps on, and her favorite toy. Don't worry about anything else. I have plenty of dog supplies, dog food and snacks here. I'll see you in a little bit." she said matter-of-factly, like she was in charge, and at that moment, she was, and that was more than fine with me. Laura was a Godsend, a life saver, and as always, a good friend.

It was so late and I was so tired, I don't remember much more of that night except that Ciccina knew. I won't say she was sad, but I will say she knew I was leaving and she was going to miss me. She kept close to me, closer than ever, if that was at all possible. On the car ride, Ciccina stayed in my lap all the way to Laura's. She stayed very still without taking any interest in anything she could possibly see out the windows, like she normally would have done. She stayed curled up and weighed heavy on my lap as if she was planting all her weight down like she did that first night when she thought I was going to pull her off of me, when I didn't want her to dirty my pants.

That time I wanted her there and wasn't going to pull her off of me. That time, I was relishing her being there with me. There wasn't too much time for sentimentality, since I had more packing to do and music to arrange, and a plane to catch. But I was missing her already too.

That week away would be the first time Ciccina and I would be out of each other's sight for more than a couple hours, and in the prior week, we had been completely inseparable. Come to think of it, I didn't take any appointments during that time or even go to the store. We were like in our own little world.

After all that, and after all those months, and after all we had been through, there I was driving to drop Ciccina off at Laura's. It was only going to be for a week, but I was still going to miss her. I knew that when I got back I would have more time to find her a good home and I wouldn't be rushed. Not that I had been rushed those past several months, but those months were for learning and for lessons, evidently. They had to be exactly what they were, I came to believe. I cherished them and the time we had together. I wouldn't have changed a thing. Well, maybe one, the "accident," but honestly, I don't know what life would have been like without that one big thing having happened.

My world had completely changed and so had Ciccina's. No one would know by looking at her, that only days earlier, she had been in a horrible accident. And from Ciccina's attitude after it all, I think it was definitely a thing of the past for her too, though I hoped she had learned many things in the process, like, to stay out of the street! As for her internal consciousness, I hope she learned that she is a beautiful and magical being and is so very loved by me.

When we arrived at Laura's, I parked and transferred Ciccina from my lap to my arms, like my Father used to do with us kids when we were asleep in the car and we had arrived home. I held Ciccina close to me all the way to Laura's door. Laura was there at the open door in her nightgown, ready to receive Ciccina with open arms.

"Hey girl, there you are. You have been through so mush, haven't you, you sweet ting." Laura spoke to Ciccina in her doggy talk, as she fawned all over her and gave her kisses. It was very special and yet in an unceremonious way, Laura had taken Ciccina into her arms and out of my hands, literally and figuratively.

As always, Ciccina was so happy to see Laura. Laura's home had become her second home. I visited Laura more often than anyone else, and would always have Ciccina with me when I did. She loved it there and she loved Laura and cherished her Laura time. Laura was extra good to her, they always had a special connection and I felt really good about leaving Ciccina with her, especially after all she had been through. And I didn't mean just what Laura meant when she said that, but everything that Laura didn't know. One thing I knew as did Laura, I knew Ciccina was going to not only be watched over, but loved.

I walked back to my car to get Ciccina's pillow, a shirt of mine, and a toy of hers, and placed them in Laura's house. Laura was still holding Ciccina and kissing her while Ciccina was licking/kissing her back. The two of them paid no attention as I came and went with things to leave behind. I had a thought that maybe, while they were not paying attention to me, I should just slip away in the hope that Ciccina wouldn't notice. I thought it might be easier on us both. But after all we had been through together, I felt like that would be deceiving her. I couldn't do that.

I wanted to give Laura a hug and a big thank you, anyway, and I did and wanted to have a moment with Ciccina. That was harder for me than I thought. If that "goodbye" had happened a week or so before, it would have been one thing, but after the week that we had had, the love that we had shared, the tears, the work, the energy, the lessons, the prayers, the miracles, that "Goodbye" was no ordinary moment. I was well aware that I was leaving Ciccina with Laura only for a week but nonetheless, it was an intense moment.

I actually kissed Ciccina on the head, something I had never done before. Maybe that was the very, very last holdout. After hugging and thanking Laura over and over again, I left two of my favorite beings in the whole world, with each other. And as I left, I said out loud, but underneath my breath, "Good bye Ciccina."

24 WHAT ARE YOUR INTENTIONS?

I caught my flight the next morning and the moment I landed, I called Laura.

"Hey Laura, how's Ciccina?" were the first words out of my mouth.

"She's fine. She's so funny, you should see her run around the house with the other dogs? We were worried about the big dog, but she's the one that chases him." she laughed.

"Run around the house?" I thought. "Chase the other dog?" After all she had been through the fact that she can do that really meant she was healed in more ways than I even imagined. "Wow," I said. Not letting on, but I was still having a hard time believing it all. That was too good to be true. What a beautiful thing.

"My friend is actually coming home early and she's picking up her dogs tonight, so it's gonna be just Ciccina and I and we're gonna have fun. I tell you, you have to change that name, she's not a Ciccina," she insisted.

We said our goodbyes and hung up the phone, but after that day, like a concerned parent, I called Laura every subsequent day afterward to ask about Ciccina. Every day Laura would have a story to tell about what Ciccina had done that day. We would laugh about each story and then Laura would say, "I'm learning a lot from her." How interesting that she should say that. Little did Laura know just how much I had learned, I thought to myself.

I would agree with her and would say, "Me too, I can't wait to tell you some stories." After one particular call, I was reminded as to how glad I was that I had not told Laura the story of Ciccina's accident. I knew I would eventually tell her, but after her loss it was too soon. At that point, it was not something I wanted to tell her over the phone and not especially while she was enjoying Ciccina as her guest. I figured I would tell her when I got back.

In every phone call I thanked Laura over and over and over again for helping me with Ciccina and she insisted that it was no trouble at all and that they were having fun. As we were getting ready to hang up, after one call in particular, Laura asked, "Before you go, I have to ask you, what did you feed her?"

I wanted to tell her that I fed her the science dog food with 100 essential vitamins and, etc., and I did feed her that, but I knew what she really liked…pasta, or anything Italian, so it seemed. I didn't reply right away except to ask, "What do you mean?"

Laura responded, "I've tried all the different dog foods that I have here and she doesn't like any of them. But the other day I sat down to eat some pasta and she was looking at me and I thought, no, you don't like pasta do you? It had garlic on it and I thought, there's no way, there's no way she's gonna eat this. Then I remember you telling me she was an Italian dog because she ate your pasta when you ate pasta, so I gave it to her, and she ate it, with the garlic on it and everything!" she shared while she laughed.

"I know," I interjected in-between my own laughter, "it's the funniest thing. She's so Italian."

"Yes, but the garlic, it was too funny. Then she was eyeing my asparagus. So I gave it to her and she loved it. She is hysterical," she laughed and laughed and I laughed too.

"I know, she's such a character, and I love her. I love you too, thanks again Laura." I said, as I rushed off the phone to get ready to go on stage. I was so happy. Ciccina deserved to be happy and in my absence, there was no one that I knew that could have taken better care of her than Laura, except maybe my Mother. Either way, Ciccina was going to be eating Italian and that was perfetto!

My week of performances went really well and flew by quickly, much quicker than the week before had, that was for sure. Guess it is true that time flies when you're having fun. I called Laura before I got on my flight and told her that I would be arriving into Los Angeles pretty late, and asked her if she wouldn't mind keeping her one more night. I thought we would all be better off if I picked up Ciccina in the morning, that was, as long as Laura was okay with it.

Laura was as gracious as always and told me not to worry and to call her in the morning and we'd figure it out from there.

When I finally got home, it was the first time that I had been home without Ciccina in months. The place was quiet and no one was there to greet me with wagging tail, and excited little jumps, and what I previously thought of as annoying kisses.

At that moment, I actually entertained the thought of keeping Ciccina. I knew it wouldn't have been possible, but I pondered it in my head, just the same. The festival season had started. I had just performed at the first in a long string of festivals I would be singing at that summer. I would be traveling quite a bit and it really would not be fair to Ciccina for me to think of keeping her. Nevertheless, the next day I was going to be picking her up and a new day was going to start and we would have to see what Ciccina and I would manifest for her as far as living arrangements. As far as that was concerned, that "goal" for that day, had still not been achieved.

The morning came and Ciccina's pillow was not in my room, and it was not in my office and it was not in my home. But I knew that it would soon be that way and that that was the right thing for Ciccina, we just had to find her the right home.

Soon after waking up I called Laura and asked her how the two of them were doing.

"We've been having a grand time," Laura said. Laura went on to tell me of some things that Ciccina had done and told me how amazing and powerful a dog she was. Laura then said something that made me pause. Laura said that Ciccina was not only a healer but a healer's dog. I wasn't sure exactly what she meant, but I knew we had never talked about the healings, so I wasn't sure how she knew Ciccina was a healer, much less a healer's dog. I asked her to explain.

Laura told me that she had had a client visit her while I was away. Laura did healing sessions with clients in her home. Evidently, while working with and on her client, at a pivotal moment, the perfect moment, Ciccina walked into the room and plopped herself on the client's lap. It was just the kind of love that the client needed for her to break down and break through some stuff that they had been working on, Laura said. She continued to tell me that, "After the client had had her breakthrough, Ciccina picked herself up and walked away. It was amazing!"

I hadn't had that experience of Ciccina, but with what I had learned about her over the past months, I could believe it. She certainly had her magic touch and Laura saw it, that's for sure.

"You know, another thing too, she loves my healing music," she said in a serious tone.

Even though she was being serious, I let out a little chuckle. In the prior months Ciccina had come to know both Marco's music and Laura's music. "Yah," Laura continued to say, "when I sing, she comes right up to me and just takes it all in, and then, when I play my recording of 'There is a Space For You,' (one of Laura's original songs), she looks like she's taking it all in," she marveled.

"I know, she's amazing." I agreed.

"Listen," Laura said as she got real serious on the phone, all of a sudden. "What are your intentions with this little one?" she asked.

"Laura, I love Ciccina, but I can't keep her. My intentions are to keep her until I find her a really special home and family, because I care about her too much and she deserves to be loved the way she loves." I said to her honestly.

"Are you sure you don't intend to keep her? After all, the two of you are so perfect together." she continued.

"Laura, I can't. Why are you asking?" I wondered.

"Well, I've been thinking," she started, "This little one needs a home." "This little one needs a home," she repeats, "and I got a home..." Then came a pregnant pause.

What was she saying? Was she asking me permission to adopt Ciccina? I had made that assumption before and had gotten excited over the thought, only to find out I had been mistaken and that was a mistake I didn't want to make again. So, I paused right along with her until neither one of us said anything for a long time.

"What are you saying?" I finally blurted out and then went back to holding my breath hoping that what she was saying was what I was wishing for both of them. It was what I had been wishing for both of them from the moment I laid eyes on Ciccina.

"Well. (pause), this little one, needs a home, (pause), and I got a home. So, I'm thinking she should stay right where she is." she finally said.

"Really? Are you serious? Oh, I am so happy!" I exclaimed.

"But!" she interrupted.

"Oh no, here comes the 'but,'" I thought to myself.

"But, if I keep her, you have to dog sit her when I go on vacation," she said.

Was she kidding me? She was telling me I could have my cake and eat it too, and was saying this was a "but" and her "condition?" From the moment I laid eyes on Ciccina I always thought she was Laura's dog. Nothing would make me happier for Ciccina's sake, for the two of them to be together. On top of which, to know that I would get to see Ciccina every time I visited Laura and to spend quality time with her when Laura went on vacation was a bonus.

"Oh Laura, I couldn't be happier. I am so happy for you and for Ciccina." I sighed.

"And we have to change her name. She's not a Ciccina." she insisted.

"Well, she's your dog now and you can call her anything you both decide," I assured her.

"Well, we'll just have to feel it out, right little one?" she said as I could hear her turning her attention to Ciccina in the background.

"You know Laura, since she is going to be your dog now, I should probably tell you what happened last week," I hesitatingly said.

I proceeded to tell Laura a very short version of the story. Basically the story was reduced to two sentences. She was in an accident and she was badly hurt on the Fourth of July.

"What? Are you kidding me? And you didn't tell me? Honey, what happened? How is she?" she said without thinking.

"Well, she's fine," I responded.

"What do you mean she's fine, she was in an accident? Did you take her to the Vet?" she questioned.

I was glad she was showing such concern. That was exactly what I would have expected from Laura, being the caring person that she is. I could tell from her reaction that she really loved Ciccina and that she had already bonded with her.

"I gotta have her checked out, we'll talk later. I'll want to hear the whole story. I gotta go." and she hung up the phone.

Upon hanging up the phone I found myself felling happy and sad at the same time. I was happy that Laura and Ciccina had finally found each other and were together. I was happy that Ciccina had found a beautiful home and new loving family with Bob, Laura's husband, and her. And I was happy that Laura again had a dog in her life that she could give love to and receive love from.

I was sad that I had caused Laura to worry. I almost wished I hadn't told her. All of a sudden all the stories that Laura had told me about being at the vets, and at the dog hospital and all the tears and the pain she experienced with her two dogs came to my mind. I remembered again why I didn't want to tell her in the first place. I didn't want her reliving those experiences and feelings again, and especially not with Ciccina.

Regardless, I knew I had done the right thing by telling Laura, since at that point Ciccina was with her, and Laura needed to know.

The next day Laura called me and told me that she had made an appointment with her vet for the day after, and was going to make sure that Ciccina was all right. Neither one of us wanted to get into the details of the story, so we didn't, but she did want to know particulars about what condition I found her in and what her "symptoms," were so she could tell the doctor.

I told her, and we both cringed and shed a couple of tears as we tried to quickly get through it for Ciccina and for both our sakes.

The next day was the day of the appointment, and I was on pins and needles all day. Had I done the right thing for Ciccina? Why had I not thought it a good idea to take her to a doctor the next day? Why had I not told anyone that might have suggested I take her to a vet? I began to second guess myself. I began to fear that the doctor might find something and Ciccina would have been suffering that whole time. I began to question everything.

Those thoughts, questions and more came flooding into my mind. Those kind of thoughts were thoughts that I had become used to thinking all my life, about anything and everything. They were all too familiar to me. But no! I was not going to go there anymore. If Ciccina had suffered through what she suffered, even if in a small part it was for me, or even if it wasn't directly for me, I was bound and determined to have learned my lesson for Ciccina and my sake. And I had learned the lessons, but old habits were dying hard.

I was determined to stay in my "knowing!" I had done what I knew at the time was the right thing to do. It was a new found knowing but it rang true for me and I felt that at every turn, I had not only Ciccina's best interest at heart and mind, but her permission, if not to boldly say, her desire.

Later in the day, Laura finally called just as she was leaving the vet. She was calling me from the car and was telling me something in a very excited voice, that I could barely understand. Between the cell phone connection and the car noise, and her excitement, I couldn't "hear" what she was saying, but I could feel her.

"Are you saying she's okay?" I asked amidst the noise and excitement.

"Yes, yes, she's fine. You did a good job. I'll call you when I'm home," she said as she disconnected the call.

I was so excited I couldn't stay seated. "Thank you, thank you, thank you," I said, over and over again. "Thank you, thank you, thank you." I was so happy for Ciccina, for Laura and for me.

I knew Laura would call me as soon as she got home but I couldn't wait to tell someone in particular, and that someone was Dorothy.

I got Dorothy on the phone and in almost as much excitement that was in Laura's voice, I too excitedly said, "Dorothy, Laura took Ciccina to the doctor and he says she's fine!"

"Well, you knew that days ago." she reminded me matter-of-factly.

"I know, but it was good to have the doctor say it," I responded.

"Well, if you needed that confirmation, then I'm glad you got it. Congratulations," she said.

Call waiting was beeping in and I knew that it was Laura, so I told Dorothy that I had to take Laura's call and got off the phone in time to answer. It was indeed Laura.

"Congratulations, you mighty healer you! You are amazing, and this little one is a miracle dog." she gushed.

"I'm so happy," I shouted out joyously.

"The doctor said that there was no way that she had been in an accident of any kind, much less one like you described it, only a week ago, especially without treatment. I told him she had treatment," and she laughed and repeated, "You're Amazing!"

"And you know what else," she said, "I was telling my Mama about her on the phone today and she asked me what I was going to call her, and I told her I wasn't sure. I then started to tell her how Italian she was and how she would love her cooking. (Laura laughs out loud). I told her about the garlic pasta. She couldn't believe it. She laughed."

Laura continued to share and at one point I heard her voice distance itself from the phone and I knew she had turned to ask Ciccina a question. I heard Ciccina bark in the background, and I knew the two of them had truly become family.

Ciccina had found a good and loving home. The final goal was achieved, and we were complete.

In that moment, all was right in the world. Laura and I eventually hung up the phone and upon doing so, a quietness and peace came over me.

Something big had happened. Something that I could not wrap my mind around in that moment. I saw glimpses of significant moments flash before my eyes. I saw Ciccina crossing the street on the first day that we lay eyes on each other. I saw Ciccina in my lap as if she had been there for many years before. I saw me trying to feed Ciccina and eventually her eating my pasta dinner. I saw Ciccina on my bed and on my couch. I saw walks around the block, parties and friends all fussing over her. I saw Fourth of July parties. I saw Ciccina running into the street. I saw Ciccina crushed. I saw her in my arms bleeding, squished and dead. I saw Ciccina running around the apartment raising her vibrations. I saw Ciccina healing. And I saw Ciccina in her new home.

After the smiles and the tears that came with the flashbacks, came a flood of lessons, thoughts and questions. I had learned about being in the moment. I had learned about patience. I had learned that there is a time for everything. I had learned that there are forms of communication much greater than those I had been taught. I learned that there is healing that some of us do not yet understand. I learned that we are powerful beyond our imagination. I learned that when the student is ready, the teacher does appear

I had experienced and learned all this from a teacher, a little dog, in fact, the little dog that could…, and did!

ACKNOWLEDGMENTS

I wish first and foremost to thank Ciccina for entering my life and teaching me that miracles can come true if you truly believe. I extend my deepest gratitude to my friends who played roles in my journey with Ciccina and pivotal roles in my life; Dorothy Lee Donahue, Laura De León, Marco Missinato, Peter Jandula-Hudson and Tricia Wall. I thank the incredible beings who are my family, without whom, I wouldn't have come to be and with whom I continue to be and grow, Mamma, Papa, Peter, Giovanna and Anthony. I thank Mark Laisure and Will Petersen for their encouragement to write and share. I thank Marnie Tenden for her edits, re-edits, design and publishing.

CPSIA information can be obtained
at www.ICGtesting.com
Printed in the USA
FSOW04n0856100517
34102FS